ProfitWorks

Alex Freytag

Speaker, Author, Entrepreneur
Expert EOS Implementer™

info@profitworksllc.com | www.profitworksllc.com

Justin —

End Entitlement!

— Alex

Stretch
Not
Snap

Create a Self-Funded Incentive Plan, End Employee Entitlement, and Get Your Vision Shared By All

Stretch Not Snap

Create a Self-Funded Incentive Plan,
End Employee Entitlement, and
Get Your Vision Shared By All

ALEX FREYTAG

ethos
collective

Printed in the United States of America

Published by Ethos Collective™
PO Box 43, Powell, OH 43065
www.ethoscollective.vip

LCCN: 2023922325
Paperback ISBN: 978-1-63680-244-2
Hardcover ISBN: 978-1-63680-245-9
e-book ISBN: 978-1-63680-246-6

Available in paperback, hardcover, e-book, and audiobook.

All EOS terms are used with permission from EOS Worldwide.

PROFITWORKS PROCESS®, PROFITWORKS SOLUTION®, THE MISSING LINK™, ADULT AGREEMENT™, TENSION TOOLS®, NO-ENTITLEMENT INCENTIVE PLAN®, PROFITLINK SOLUTION®, PROFITWORKS®, PROFITLINK MASTERCLASS™ are owned by In Tension LLC dba ProfitWorks®. Used with permission.

All illustrations by Alex Freytag.

OTHER BOOKS BY ALEX FREYTAG

www.stretchnotsnap.com

"Every work contains a lifetime of experience."
—Rick Rubin

CONTENTS

FOREWORD

Entrepreneurs come in all shapes and sizes. Entrepreneurial businesses are vital for the global economy as they provide the goods and services that enable us to live the lives we all want. Without the innovations provided to us by entrepreneurs, we would still be hunting and gathering, freezing to death by our fires in the winter and sweating at night in the summer. Entrepreneurs have created abundance in our world by taking resources to higher and higher productivity levels.

Abundance in the world can only occur with the collaboration and coordination of many people in and outside the confines of entrepreneurial businesses. So, what makes people want to cooperate to achieve massive, abundance-creating goals? Incentives.

We are all motivated by incentives, whether we acknowledge it or not. We do what's in our best interests, and then once we are satisfied, we move on to creating abundance for our families, our communities, and beyond. Incentives are the basis for the study of behavioral economics.

What you'll read in this book is the simplest and most effective way to leverage behavioral economics to get what you want from your business and help your employees get what they want simultaneously. If you follow what Alex Freytag suggests in this book, you will align human energy in your company faster and more effectively than you ever thought possible.

Implementing the Entrepreneurial Operating System® (EOS®) is the first step in aligning human energy in your business. Your people will be on the same page with your vision and more accountable and healthy than ever. But that's only the first step. If you want to align ALL the human energy in your business, you must harness the power of human nature with incentives.

As an Expert EOS Implementer™, EOS Community Leader, and co-founder of the EOS Conference®, you will learn from one of the most dedicated entrepreneurial servants I know. I've known Alex for the better part of a decade. He possesses a gift to simplify complex ideas and help implement them. This book is no different. Alex has a passion for seeing you win.

As you follow Swan Services into its next phase of aligning human energy, I encourage you to pay close attention to the story's genius and the lessons taught. If you do, you will get what you want from your business, and your people will get what they want from their lives. Everyone will feel more motivated, excited, and fulfilled while working for your company.

When aligning human energy around your vision, know that content without context does more harm than good. What I love about this book is that it will help you give your people the *context* they need to understand how your business works and how they contribute to the success of the company, their team, and themselves. By context, I mean gifting your people the financial education they need to make better decisions that drive the company forward.

EOS Implementers have worked directly with over 20,000 leadership teams and more than ten times that are using our tools to get more of what they want from their businesses. I hope all of them take the next step in harnessing the power of human nature by implementing the powerful tools described in this book.

While reading this book, consider your people as little balls of energy. Your job as a leader is to harness those energy balls and get them rolling in the same direction. If anything gets in the way of focusing that power, it will slow you down. Organizations of all types waste time and energy trying to align their people.

You may be trying all sorts of engagement surveys, team-building events, state-of-the-company addresses, and many other initiatives to get all your people rowing in the same direction. If you are doing everything necessary to align your people and get your vision Shared By All but have missed incentives, you've come to the right place.

Thinking about incentive plans can make you stressed and worried about how you will pay for and implement them. Alex takes the stress out by designing incentive plans that are self-funding and enduring and eliminate entitlement.

Your business, like every business, is unique. There's no one-size-fits-all way to educate and incentivize your people. This book will give you the framework and the mindsets you need to get your people what they want so you can get what you want.

Mark O'Donnell
Visionary at EOS Worldwide
December 2023

NOTE TO THE READER

Fanfiction novels are stories written by fans featuring characters, settings, and plots from a particular novel. *Stretch Not Snap* is just such a fable. If you've read *Get A Grip* by Gino Wickman and Mike Paton, you are no doubt familiar with the fictitious company Swan Services and the Visionary/Integrator duo of Vic and Eileen.

Stretch Not Snap tells a continuation story of these characters and their entrepreneurial company that is running on EOS (The Entrepreneurial Operating System). This fable occurs several years after starting the EOS Process®, and Swan is gaining traction. However, they are still frustrated by a sense of entitlement that exists among their employees. Swan offers discretionary annual bonuses that have become expected holiday gifts, but they lack employees who are "ownership thinkers," and the company vision is not yet truly internalized by everyone.

Though fictional, *Stretch Not Snap* is a real-world story about an entrepreneurial company poised to move to the next level. They're having good meetings, they have their priorities straight, and the leadership team is aligned on the vision. The company is gaining traction because they've been running on EOS for a few years, but they're frustrated by this entitlement mentality and by a lack of true engagement among the employees. The employees hear the vision, but they don't really see or feel connected to the vision at all. They don't all believe in the vision. And most importantly, they don't know how they individually contribute to the vision—there is a weak link between what they do every day and the company's vision.

The company has a system for tackling "people issues" when they arise, and through meeting with Eddie Stevens, their ProfitWorks guide, they understand that an incentive plan won't solve all these people issues. They must handle those using the tools that they've been provided through EOS. Companies like Swan Services, who are running on EOS, might choose any number of methods to incentivize and engage their people in a way that allows them to attract and retain great people. This story illustrates just one of those options.

As you read this, a heads-up that you will encounter many EOS-specific terms. If you are unfamiliar with these terms, I suggest adding the business book *Traction* by Gino Wickman to your reading list. This is the first book in the Traction library and was published prior to *Get A Grip*. Reading the *Get A Grip* entrepreneurial fable, in addition, will also certainly provide more context. Either way, I have tried to spell out the EOS terms within the body of this book, and ideally, the context within which the terms are used should give you a sense of their definition.

A little background for you: Since 1996, I've personally taken hundreds of companies through the ProfitWorks Process® described in this story. Although this book is a fable, I hope these realistic characters and familiar situations help you see how to solve the most important and common incentive plan, culture, and people engagement issues you face as a leader. The practical tools discussed in the book will help you create a culture of employees who think and act like owners. I'm confident they will because, over and over again, I've seen that the results of implementing the ProfitWorks Solution® are truly remarkable. But don't take my word for it; listen as other entrepreneurs speak for themselves:

> "In *Stretch Not Snap*, Alex has done a great job building on what Paton and I created in *Get A Grip*. This book is insightful and demystifies the journey from entitlement mentality to a rewarding workplace of ownership and engagement. It will help entrepreneurs develop employees who truly share their vision."
>
> *Gino Wickman*
> *Author of Traction & Shine,*
> *Creator of EOS*

> "In *Stretch Not Snap*, Alex Freytag tells a compelling story using the characters from *Get A Grip*, the business fable Gino Wickman and I first published in 2012. He and our old friends at Swan Services tackle a common problem for entrepreneurial leaders – building a great culture full of highly motivated employees who want to help their company achieve its vision. You'll laugh, you may cry (people can be frustrating) – and you'll learn how to replace a "me first" mindset with a team of champions intent on winning together."
>
> *Mike Paton*
> *Author of Process! and Get A Grip*

> "*Stretch Not Snap* describes an amazing and simple methodology to create incentive plans designed to truly drive team engagement, financial results and help entrepreneurial companies get everything they

want from their business! I was drawn in by this fun and informative fable and look forward to how it will strengthen our team at EOS Worldwide!"

Kelly Knight
Integrator, EOS Worldwide

"This book addresses something all companies struggle with----designing incentive plans that work! Alex does a masterful job engaging the reader in an easy-reading fable, but one that offers real-life solutions that will increase bottom line performance for any organization."

Jim Zink
Visionary, Zink Corporation

"*Stretch Not Snap* is a compelling narrative that offers valuable insights into designing an incentive plan that fosters employee engagement and instills a sense of ownership. This ultimately benefits not only your bottom line but also enriches the lives of your employees."

Rob Dube
Visionary, The 10 Disciplines

"In *Stretch Not Snap*, Alex Freytag artfully weaves a tale in parable format that not only captivates the reader but also drives home an essential lesson for modern businesses: the power of financial literacy among employees. This book sheds light on the transformative impact of equipping team members with the tools they need to understand and shape a company's financial destiny. But it doesn't stop there. This parable beautifully ties in the benefits of sharing the fruits of a company's success with those who contributed to it: the employees. By illustrating the profound effects of profit-performance bonuses, Freytag offers a convincing case that when employees are educated, motivated, and rewarded in line with a company's success, the possibilities are boundless. *Stretch Not Snap* is aptly named, revealing that the right kind of pressure can forge stronger team bonds, cultivate mutual investment, and yield unprecedented results in the business world."

Casey Brown
President and Visionary, Boost Pricing

"*Stretch Not Snap* speaks directly to my own experience in launching our company's first-ever No-Entitlement Incentive Plan®. When paired with the specific implementation steps discussed in Alex's book, *Profit Works*, I have a really clear path forward. Launching an incentive plan can seem insurmountable, but *Stretch Not Snap* really helped ease my anxiety around launching our plan. I now see my own tension around launching our plan as Positive Tension!"

Michael Whalen
President, PlayCare

"Simple. Practical. Actionable. Alex has tackled a challenge faced by nearly all entrepreneurs: Getting employees to think and act like owners. Through vivid and realistic storytelling, he has illustrated a clear and simple path to creating an ownership culture. This book will be required reading for all of my leadership teams."

John Ward
Certified EOS Implementer®

"After watching hundreds of business owners over the past quarter century create more bad than good with profit sharing and bonus schemes, Alex comes to the rescue. Every sentence in this book makes sense, and every business owner, manager, and head of finance should read it before making very common and costly decisions that are potentially devastating to employee morale."

Kevin G Armstrong
Author, TEDx Speaker, Expert EOS Implementer

"I LOVE this book! In this engaging and well-told story, *Stretch Not Snap* outlines exactly what you need to do to go from having a culture of entitlement to one of ownership, productivity, and increased profitability. A must-read for the committed business owner who wants to bring out the very best in their team and reap the rewards."

Shannon Waller
Entrepreneurial Team Strategist, Strategic Coach

"For years, I've struggled to create a culture of ownership thinking. This book is a quick read and has helped me create financial literacy in my organization. For the first time, I feel we have the framework for a win-win plan and can effectively move from bonusing to profit sharing."

Megan Shroy
Visionary, Approach Marketing

"Tired of everyone getting a trophy for just showing up? Me too! If you're an entrepreneur frustrated with entitlement mentality, this book will inspire you to create a compensation structure that builds on the culture of discipline and accountability you have always wanted."

Scott Rusnak
Expert EOS Implementer
Author, Board Certified Coach USA Cycling &
Team Great Britain

"*Stretch Not Snap*, along with Alex Freytag's *Profit Works*, are books we share with our Fractional CFO clients. The foundational concepts and disciplines upon which ProfitWorks is built are a shared, common core to how FocusCFO works with clients to achieve a business of greater, transferrable value, and which meets the goals of owners and employees alike. The parable style of *Stretch Not Snap* introduces the concepts of a 'no entitlement' incentive plan in an easily digestible format to help leaders relate them to their specific businesses. And forms a natural lead-in to the implementation steps found in *Profit Works*."

Michael Stier
Area President & Director of Marketing, FocusCFO

"No more entitled team members. No more failed bonus programs. Strengthen your culture and your profit line by leveraging Alex's powerful yet simple approach to a self-funded incentive plan. Everyone wins when profit targets are hit. It's a great strategy to retain 'A' players too!!"

Justin Maust
EOS Implementer®

"Alex has hit a home run when it comes to simplifying concepts that can be intimidating even to business owners and their leadership teams. *Stretch Not Snap* is a must-read for any business owner who is serious about maximizing their organization's potential. Potential to increase profitability, yes, but most importantly, to leverage the effectiveness of an Operating System in order to allow every employee to understand, connect, and contribute to the results. In my 9 years of guiding and coaching teams implementing EOS, fully embracing a shared future that includes a healthy balance between 'Me and We' can be one of the most elusive objectives. Alex paints a clear and simple path for all of us to follow."

John McMahon
EOS Implementer

"This is THE book for every family business owner who is afraid to share their revenue and profit numbers with their team. It outlines how to share the numbers and what the risks are if you keep them secret."

Sara B. Stern
EOS Implementer and Family Business Fanatic

"Many business owners avoid the idea of developing compensation plans due to fear or lack of understanding. Alex takes the complexity out of compensation plans. He gives you practical tools and actions you can use to design a plan that works for your team. It's simple to understand and explain, all while helping your best team members level up."

Aaron Purkeypile
EOS Implementer

"*Stretch Not Snap* served as an important reminder for us to ensure that our business operating system and team health were strong before launching a new incentive system in our organization. With that foundation in place, the book shares tangible examples of how we can begin climbing up the positive tension curve by sharing data and profit-focused training to help eradicate entitlement mentality. *Stretch Not Snap* will be a go-to resource throughout the ages to help me strive for my business to flow from Me to We using these beneficial tools and principles."

Sandy King
President, Symbiont Service

"As we were transitioning to an ESOP, we needed a partner to help coach us in creating a new incentive plan design that supported our new 'employee ownership' culture. ProfitWorks supported us with easy-to-use educational tools that taught our employees how their daily activities link directly to driving Giroux's performance and, ultimately, to self-funding their own profit-sharing plan."

Nataline Lomedico
CEO/President, Giroux Glass

"Many so-called leaders and managers pin the label of 'entitlement' on specific people or generations, but it is actually these 'leaders' causing the problem because they do not have the energy, awareness, guts, courage, or moxie to adopt a systematic way to create and maintain what my friend Alex is calling positive tension. Alex is describing the Goldilocks zone that we work so hard to help our EOS clients create and advance: not too hot, not too cold, just the right amount of tension that builds amazing cultures and delivers excellent repeatable results. Understanding *Stretch Not Snap* is critical if you intend to fully reap the rewards of your investment in EOS."

Walt Brown
Seasoned, Multi-company Entrepreneur,
Author of The Patient Organization, Attract or
Repel, Death of the Org Chart,
Expert EOS Implementer

This book and the ProfitWorks Solution are designed not just to give you something to think about. They're thorough enough to help you and your leadership team fully implement these tools and achieve results like those of the companies above. For many readers, observing a company actually implementing the ProfitWorks Solution will make the process easier to follow and apply. It also provides greater insights into the realities of implementation. For those readers who want the nuts-and-bolts guide to the ProfitWorks Solution, my prior book, *Profit Works*, offers a practical guide to implementation.

When I decided to write this book, it was a true passion project. As I started to write, the words and situations flowed out of me because I help entrepreneurial teams at small to midsize companies realize untapped potential every day. This book is based on hundreds of true stories.

I've tried to encapsulate my nearly three decades of work in this field into this simple fable. Early on, my brother and I toiled for over 6 years without a paycheck, honing and refining many business literacy concepts I share in this book. These timeless concepts have been around for hundreds of years and will probably be around for a thousand more because this is just how businesses work. Through that early work, we found that when employees begin to understand the entrepreneurial mindset, especially as it relates to the risk-return equation, they are a bit more sympathetic to our entrepreneurial reality. They want to be around that environment because it's fun, it's exciting, and there's an element of risk, danger, and uncertainty to it. But also, because they're not the ones taking all the risk, they have a sense of confidence in the role they play in helping your business.

Risk is not easy for most people to stomach. In Gino Wickman's book *Entrepreneurial Leap*, he describes Risk as one of the 6 essential traits for an entrepreneur. As an entrepreneur, I've never really felt like I've been taking risks because I was so sure of the ideas that I was acting on. If you're an entrepreneur, you know what I'm talking about. But this risk, which is arguably part of one's DNA, is on somewhat of a spectrum. The risk-return equation is such an easy concept to wrap our heads around, but in my experience, most employees are not aware of it. It's not something that's taught in schools generally, and other basic financial literacy concepts, such as balancing a checkbook, are also often overlooked as we parent our children to financial freedom.

The incentive plan is not the focus of what I'm teaching in this book, but it's the topic that most business owners gravitate toward because it can be such a complex issue. It's certainly something we are trying to simplify, but it's my experience that incentives are not a panacea; they are just one tool in your leadership toolbox.

In the next phase of my evolution, through my work as a partner at a company called Ownership Thinking, I was able to build on these basic business literacy concepts and my philosophy and experience around the impact and subtlety of incentive plans in organizations. The companies that have purely implemented the concepts I discuss in this book find that they have a lot more fun on their journey to growing their businesses. They tend to be very profitable, and those owners truly get a high out of returning some of those well-earned profits back to the team that helped them.

In this book, I describe an online business literacy Masterclass. My vision is to include a lot more content than what I describe in this book. My goal is to partner with other content providers, experts, and teachers who want to help employees see a much bigger picture and a much brighter future for themselves. In my experience, when employees really begin to see your vision and truly share your vision, their confidence goes up, and they become interested in creating their own vision of financial freedom for themselves and their families. It's up to us as Leaders to provide the tools, training, and resources for them to become active participants in getting out of the entitlement zone and moving into their own version of an earning zone.

The natural fear that arises when we try to encourage people to move out of entitlement comes from that risk that the guide, Eddie Stevens, talks about in this book. There is a risk to discussing tough topics in a conversation with a peer or a boss. There is a risk to having healthy conflict. There is a risk to asking more from your employees and implementing Tension Tools® like Scorecards, measurables, core values, and other tools that create higher expectations of performance.

But that risk can have an enormous payoff, not only for you as an entrepreneur in your business, through providing returns for you, but also in the form of a more completely appreciative employee, one who is able to see the bigger picture, and who can lead their own life pursuing their own personal vision. Entrepreneurship can be lonely, as you may have experienced. And this path is an endeavor of love and of really caring about people. And this can make a huge difference.

Think about your ultimate goal as an entrepreneur. Do you want more freedom? Do you want to make more money? Get more time back? Perhaps create a great culture with great people and great results, like the characters in this fable have chosen to strive for? I believe *Stretch Not Snap* will help you gain all these things. My passion is being a hero to entrepreneurs. I want to help you get everything you want out of your business. I know this book will help you get to the next level, not only around the performance of your business and the engagement of your employees but also around helping you create a more fulfilling and impactful life for yourself and your team.

If you need more resources or want to connect with us, please visit StretchNotSnap.com. For now, start reading, enjoy the story, and begin the process of truly creating a culture of ownership thinkers.

CHAPTER 1

ENTITLEMENT MENTALITY

Eileen stared out the window of her office, thinking about the last few hours at the company's quarterly State of the Company Meeting. They had 100 percent attendance this time, which was a first. The news they shared about where the company has been over the last quarter, where it is now year-to-date, and where they are going revealed some pretty good news about Swan Services.

It was when they opened it up for questions that the meeting took a major left turn.

Vic, her Visionary, had gone through the Vision page of the company's Vision/Traction Organizer®, or V/TO®, and finished painting a beautiful picture of where the company would be in three short years. Eileen took over from there and walked through the Traction side of the tool.

The 1-Year Plan she shared was an exciting prediction of the upcoming year. They predicted revenues of $10 million with a profit of 12 percent. They were targeting the creation of 40 new big projects over $100K. At no time in their history had they ever even sniffed these types of numbers.

Since implementing EOS with Alan Roth a few years back and graduating from him as their EOS Implementer, she and Vic had successfully taken the reins of communicating the tools deeper into the company.

There was something missing, though. As Eileen gazed out across the team of 35 souls and considered how they were receiving all this company information, she realized that this felt like her information. This was her and Vic's company, not theirs. This meeting was a one-way presentation of information. It was tactical, and it seemed cold. There was no emotion in the delivery.

It appeared to Eileen that although they *heard* her and Vic, they didn't really *feel* like they had a part in generating all this information. It seemed like they didn't understand that their efforts, choices, and behavior could create all the data: the growth, the drive, the wins, and the big projects. Even though Vic and Eileen owned the company, it really was the *team's company*, all of them, including Vic and Eileen. How could she help them feel this? She wanted them to feel the excitement that she and Vic felt for Swan's potential. Their eyes, though, seemed to express fear and doubt more than anything else.

Perhaps in this instance, SBA on the Vision Component® of the EOS Model® stood for Scared By All instead of Shared By All.

As they opened the meeting up to questions, there was an awkward silence. Vic asked, "Are you sure you guys don't have any questions?" They waited.

Evan, from operations, raised his hand, and Vic pointed to him. "Thanks, Evan, get us started."

"Ten million dollars is more than we have ever done, right?" Evan asked.

"That's right," said Vic.

"I don't know if we have enough people in Ops to get that amount of work out the door. Will we be hiring?" Evan asked.

"Good question," said Vic. "We're looking at The Accountability Chart™, especially in Tom's area, Ops, and keeping an eye on open seats. This quarter, we do have some Rocks around hiring to make sure we have the resources to keep up."

Eileen added, "Evan, we're also watching the number of proposals and the probability of closing those proposals so we can respond faster when we see our funnel filling up. With our weekly meetings, we should be able to predict better and faster and make moves in alignment with the big projects that close. Does that answer your question?"

Evan nodded, "Thanks."

Kevin, an IT consultant, raised his hand.

"Kevin?" said Vic.

"This looks great, Vic and Eileen. One question I have that maybe others do, too: Do you know when we'll be getting our annual bonuses?"

Vic answered quickly, "Thanks, Kevin. We're not quite sure. Eileen and I are working on it. Could be a few weeks."

Kevin said, "Okay, just curious because my wife and I are traveling over the holidays, and we could really use the cash."

A few others nodded.

"Yeah, if we did $8 million this year, we should get some pretty hefty bonuses, right?" asked Blair.

"Well, just because we delivered $8 million in top-line revenue doesn't mean we have $8 million," Eileen calmly said while trying to mask her frustration. "There are a lot of expenses we have to cover with that. And we're keeping an eye on cash as well."

"What other questions do you guys have before we get back to it?" asked Vic. There were no more hands up, so he adjourned the meeting.

• • •

After the meeting, Todd came into Eileen's office. "Hey, you got a second, Eileen?" Todd worked in engineering and reported to Tom in operations.

"What's up?" said Eileen.

"Hey, I'm kind of concerned, and I guess I wanted to vent a little if that's okay," he answered.

"Sure, what's going on?" Eileen asked, more concerned now. "Sit down, Todd," she said, looking at the clock.

"Well, I went to lunch with a few of the team members, and they were talking about the bonuses last year."

Eileen nodded.

Todd continued. "Well, Sheila said she got $5,000 last year, and I think she thought we all got the same thing. I know I didn't get anything near that amount, and we do the same kind of work."

"Yeah, Vic and I have been talking about this bonus situation, and we haven't figured it all out yet. Rest assured, though, Todd. We had a decent year last year, like we said in the State of the Company meeting, and we'll be communicating what's going on with bonuses very soon."

"How did we do?" asked Todd. "I mean, like how much did we make?"

"Well, we hit our one-year sales goal, we actually surpassed it by a little, in fact. Profit was good, too."

"I don't really know how profit works, but I've heard you talk about profit being around 50 percent. Is that what you and Vic basically take home?

"No!" Eileen blurted out, concerned. "Oh shoot, I've got a call coming up, Todd. I wish I could go deeper into this right now . . . that 50 percent is called 'gross profit,' and it's what's left over after we pay all our *direct* expenses, which is mostly labor. From that, the company still must pay other costs like rent, salaries, insurance, administrative costs, and so forth. I'm so sorry, I gotta jump on this call."

Eileen's brain was swimming with concern now. "Let's do this: I'll get with Vic and put our heads together on year-end bonuses, and I commit to you that we'll communicate something in the next seven days. Will that work for you?"

Todd said, "Of course, I'll let you get going. Hey Eileen, is there anything I can read that will help me understand more about this stuff?"

Eileen said she didn't know but that she'd think about it.

After her call, Eileen bee-lined straight to Vic's office. "Vic, we've got to talk about bonuses ASAP," she said as she burst through his door. "There's some really inaccurate information floating around about how much you and I really make. I think everyone thinks we're making wheelbarrows full of money!"

"Well, I am. I thought you were, too," Vic said with a sly grin.

"You know what, Vic? That kind of attitude is gonna eventually get us in trouble." Eileen was smiling, but Vic knew she was serious. "I know you're kidding around, but if anyone heard you, I really think you could do damage to the culture. Word gets around, you know."

"I know, I know, Eileen."

The smile faded as Eileen continued. "And we've got fairness issues with some of the team sharing with each other what they got last year!"

"Who shared what?" Vic asked.

"Todd pulled me aside and let me know a few of the team were talking at lunch about what each of them got last year. You'll recall that we juiced up Sheila's bonus because she did so well with that project late last year, and she apparently shared that information with a few others." Eileen paused for a moment to compose herself before continuing. "You pair that with the fact that Kevin's potentially already spent the money on his vacation, and he has no idea why he's getting it—there's no tie between the bonus and what he's doing every day. I'm telling you, Vic, our current bonus situation is not working to our advantage."

"I agree," said Vic. "What do you think we should do about it?"

"I'm not sure." She paused to consider their options. "There's a speaker at my roundtable tomorrow talking about compensation and incentive plans. I'll take good notes and see if maybe there are some nuggets I can bring back."

"That would be great," Vic said. "Let me know. It seems like we shouldn't keep doing the annual spreadsheet thing to calculate bonuses for everyone. Now that the company is starting to hockey stick, we should probably get more disciplined about it. Can you add it to our Same Page issues list? By the way, when is our next Same Page Meeting®?"

"Let's see . . . Monday is the first Monday of the month, so it's next Monday. Let's catch up then."

"Sounds good. And let me know what the guy says about bonuses."

CHAPTER 2

THE GUIDE

Eileen pulled briskly into the parking lot of Three Trees, where the business roundtable was being held. It was 7:50 am, and she was running later than she liked, but she was still on time.

As she entered the reception area, the receptionist was talking on the phone. After she made eye contact, she mouthed, "Roundtable?" The woman motioned with her head to the sign by the inside door that directed people for the event to go upstairs. Eileen nodded and quickly headed upstairs. As she approached the room, she slowed her pace, caught her breath, and smoothed her clothes before entering. The business roundtable Executive Director Bill Pullian and several of the other members, including Miguel, Julia, and John, were chatting and enjoying bagels, coffee, and juice.

Eileen helped herself to a bagel and a cup of coffee and found a seat. The group made small talk for a few minutes while others arrived, and at 8 o'clock, Bill stood up to quiet everyone down and kicked off the meeting.

"Good morning, everyone," said Bill. "It's our last meeting of the year, and I think this one is quite timely, considering how many companies struggle with bonus plans and compensation systems. Our speaker today is Eddie

Stevens from a company called ProfitWorks. He is going to talk with us about Incentive Plans and developing an Ownership Culture. I will let him tell you about himself, so, Eddie, the floor is yours."

"Thank you, Bill. Thank you very much for having me. I am excited to be here and look forward to working with you today. As Bill said, I am Eddie Stevens, and my company is ProfitWorks. Our topic today is 'Unraveling the Complexity of Incentive Plans.'

"In my experience, most incentive plans don't work. They don't do what they're supposed to do. So, we'll talk about that and how to avoid the problems I see in a lot of plans. First, I'd like to start by going around the room and asking each of you to introduce yourself and just give me a short elevator speech about your company. For example, mine is, 'We help people realize untapped potential by creating cultures of employees who think and act like owners.'"

Each member of the group introduced themselves and gave Eddie a brief overview of their role and their company.

When the last person finished, Eddie started again. "Great. Thank you for doing that. It's nice to meet you, and I appreciate the invitation to speak with your group. I want to start by telling you a little about ProfitWorks, our background, and how we got started. Then, we'll dive into the different components of the ProfitWorks Solution. We'll have a few interactive exercises, and I'll show you a video later this morning. We'll take two breaks along the way as well. If you have questions along the way, please just raise your hand, and I'll try to answer it the best I can."

Everyone nodded attentively.

"ProfitWorks is a small company, but we have a very large footprint. Our clients come from all across the country. We have partners in Canada, and we do some work internationally as well. We do a lot of public speaking;

between my partner and me, we talk to almost 100 different groups each year, so we're able to touch a lot of people with our mission. To date, we have helped nearly 500 companies implement this way of doing business over the last 27 years. When we first started doing this, it was bleeding edge; now, it is safe to say it is leading edge. The best companies do business this way.

"It's important to think of ProfitWorks not as a program and not as a motivational seminar, but rather as a way of doing business. It's a model for driving business results with a highly unified, business-literate culture, and in my experience, it is hands-down the best way to run a business.

"As I mentioned, we've been doing this for a long time, and we've developed an incredible community of companies—very forward-thinking companies—that like to share and grow. And these companies do incredibly well: It's not uncommon for our clients to achieve significant profit improvements within a year or two after implementing ProfitWorks. So, financially, it is great, but the other benefit, and the one that's more difficult to measure, is the cultural impact on your business. When you go down this path, and your employees begin to understand the financial impact of their decisions, they start making better decisions and becoming better leaders; they're more accountable, and they drive each other in a positive way. It has an incredible impact on your culture.

"Also, when your employees understand the financial impact of their decisions, they start to understand how your company 'keeps score.' Now, when you think about your businesses, how do you, well, how does any company keep score?"

Eddie paused, allowing the audience to think about the question. Another moment went by, and it was clear he wanted someone to throw some ideas out.

"Profit," said one member.

"Sales," said Amy.

"Sure, profit and sales help us. Where do you find these measures?" asked Eddie to the group.

"P&L?" said Fred.

"Exactly," said Eddie. "The P&L, also known as the Income Statement, is one of the financial statements all organizations use to track their sales, costs, and profits. So, companies use financial statements to keep score. The income statement, the balance sheet, and the cash flow statement are the three statements, right?

"Now, there are some significant problems with using *only* financial statements to run your business—what do you think they are?"

Again, Eddie paused to allow the audience to think about the question.

"No one understands them," said Jane.

"Right," said Eddie. "Many people don't understand them. I work with a lot of companies, and I even see people on leadership teams who don't understand financial statements. I'm not being critical; it's just that if you grow up in a sales role and you're a great sales manager, it doesn't make you a financial whiz, right? If you're a great operations guy, it doesn't mean you're a financial whiz.

"So, we've got one drawback to using just financial statements to drive your business—most people don't understand them." Eddie wrote *1) No understanding* on the whiteboard, then asked, "What's another problem?"

PROBLEMS w/ FINANCIAL STATEMENTS:
1) NO UNDERSTANDING

The members thought for a moment, and when no one offered an idea, Eddie said, "When do you get financial statements?"

"After the month is over," said Martha.

"That's right," said Eddie. "The key word is 'after.' It's too late to do anything about it. Financial statements don't tell you anything about what happened along the way; they just tell you the score at the end of the game. But if I don't understand the financial impact of my decisions along the way, I can't improve the 'runs, hits, errors.' So, that's a second drawback: the financials are historical information; they're lagging indicators. It's too late to do anything about them."

Eddie wrote *2) Too late* on the whiteboard.

PROBLEMS w/ FINANCIAL STATEMENTS:
1) NO UNDERSTANDING
2) TOO LATE

Eddie continued. "The last issue I see is that, even if you are sharing detailed financial information with your workforce, would everyone understand how they contributed to the financial results they are looking at?"

Most members shook their heads.

"By the way, I am not recommending that we share detailed financial statements with all our employees. I am not necessarily advocating 'open-book management.' Have you heard of open-book management?"

Some of the members nodded.

"For those of you who don't know, open-book management is a system of management in which a company regularly shares detailed financial information with all employees. In my experience, though, a company can share some level of information. In fact, share as much information as you are comfortable sharing if it will help people focus on the right measurables. As you get more comfortable and they start to understand, you can share more. I think you can make incredible progress with some of the tools we'll talk about today, which does not require 'opening the books' to all employees. To be frank, that can freak a lot of business owners out.

"We were starting to talk about this weak link between what employees do every day, their leading activities, and the financial statements they may see from time to time, which show lagging measures. People show up every day at work and do their jobs. They are generally mired in the details, and when the company shares bigger picture results with them, they often don't know what they did to contribute to the financial performance. This weak link is the third issue I see with using just financial information to drive company performance."

Eddie wrote *3) Weak link* on the whiteboard.

PROBLEMS w/ FINANCIAL STATEMENTS:
1) NO UNDERSTANDING
2) TOO LATE
3) WEAK LINK

"So, we can see that using only financial statements to run your business has some limitations. And that leads to the question, what is it that creates financial performance in your company? Think about your organization. When you boil it all down, what creates financial performance?"

Eddie paused.

The group was thinking about it.

"Sales?" Fred offered.

"Quality," said John.

"What creates sales? What creates quality?" asked Eddie.

"People," said a few of the members in unison.

"That's exactly right," said Eddie. "In my opinion, two things create financial performance in any organization: the people and all the stuff they do. If we really want to engage our employees in improving the financial performance of our company, what we really need to focus on are these measurables, these leading activity-based indicators. These are the measurables that will have the most significant financial impact on your organization, and we want to engage our employees to manage them proactively. And we want to take it a step further. I have always liked comparing business to a game. Why do we play games?"

"To win," said Dexter.

"That's right," said Eddie. "To win that competitive piece. And there's something else, something along the way?"

"To have fun," said Martha.

"Sure, and I think we can all agree, it's a lot more fun when you're winning!"

Some of the members laughed.

"We're going to build a Scorecard together to track these measurables, and we'll put people's names on the Scorecard. We will get together weekly, in meetings with our teams, to forecast or predict and discuss those leading measurables on a regular and formal basis so we can be proactive. By doing this, we'll create an environment where we're telling each other what we're *going* to do: a culture of high visibility. When you have high visibility, what else do you have?"

"Accountability?" offered Amy.

"That's right, accountability because you can't hide . . . but we don't want to create a culture of fear where we have blame and finger pointing. We want to create an environment of learning—a positive culture—where people are growing, participating, and helping each other. We're going to talk about how to do that today."

Eddie momentarily held each person's gaze to make sure everyone was with him.

"So, imagine this: You've taught everyone in your company about business. You've given them tools like Scorecards, measurables, a meeting discipline, and tools like Challenge Rocks, which we'll talk about later today. They will absolutely become actively involved in growing your business, and what do you think will happen to the profitability?" he paused.

"It'll increase," said Jane.

"That's right! Like I said, in many companies, it will more than double in less than a year! This is very common with companies that go down this path.

"So that's when we think about an incentive plan, which is the second element of the ProfitWorks Solution. You have this pot of money you've never had before, and you are able to comfortably share some of it with your employees because the incentive plan will actually pay for itself. It is *self-funding*! That's one of the most important aspects of any incentive plan you develop for your company: It has to pay for itself. In fact, if you design an incentive plan that doesn't pay for itself, what have you created in your business?"

"An expense?" asked Eileen.

"An entitlement," said Miguel.

"Yes, both of those things," said Eddie. "I don't know anyone who is looking to create more expenses in their company. And entitlement mentality is a disease. We'll talk today about how to create effective incentive plans that really work to shape employee behavior to direct their human energy so that they don't become entitlements.

"So, we've spent a lot of time building a model we can replicate in any industry. We help companies implement this way of doing business every day."

Eileen was feeling really good about this speaker. Already, Eddie had made her think about the bonuses that she and Vic were wrestling with back at the office. If they paid them out as they were planning, she knew the employees wouldn't connect the dots to really understand what they did to earn that money. She had to admit anything they paid out would be considered a gift, an entitlement. These payouts certainly weren't driving improved financial performance at Swan. It was a missed opportunity, for sure.

CHAPTER 3

POSITIVE TENSION

Eileen's mind was already spinning with Eddie's ideas and applying them to Swan. She came into the meeting feeling hopeful but somewhat deflated because of the current situation at Swan. Her thoughts were interrupted when Eddie continued.

"The ProfitWorks philosophy has at its foundation a concept called Positive Tension. Positive Tension is based on the Yerkes-Dodson law, which was developed in 1908 by two guys named Yerkes and Dodson. What Yerkes and Dodson discovered is that there is a direct relationship between tension and performance. They realized that pressure or tension is on a continuum. If you remember the X & Y axes from math class in high school, the X-axis or the horizontal axis, we'll call 'Tension.'"

Eddie drew a horizontal line on the whiteboard.

"And you can plot tension on a continuum from low to high. Low is here on the left side of the line, and high is over here on the right. And the Y-axis, or the vertical axis, we'll call 'Performance.'"

Eddie was drawing as he was talking.

"You have this chart in your handout, and what I'd like you to do is draw the curve along with me in your workbook as we're talking about this.

"They discovered that when there's no tension, when there's not much asked of people, or there are no stated expectations of performance, basically people generally just show up, punch the clock, work, and go home. There tend to be lower levels of performance. As tension is stretched in the organization, performance increases, up to a point, and then it declines."

Eddie had drawn a bell curve.

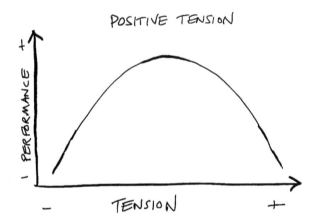

"Check this out. I've got this rubber band here. Here it is: no structure, no tension, no stretch. When there is no tension, bottom left of this curve," he said, pointing to the whiteboard, "there is low performance, right? This rubber band doesn't really do much good when there's no tension. But as you increase the tension, well, you could put it around blueprints, you could put it around some photos, or a poster, a bunch of pens, and so forth, and it gets useful, right?

"Yerkes-Dodson discovered this kind of bell curve that shows that as tension increases, performance increases. It's pretty cool. Of course, if you stretch the rubber band too far, it'll snap, so there is a balance that is required. Just enough tension. Stretching without snapping.

"So that's the premise for this. In a drive towards simplification, let's label these. We'll do three zones. On the left, and please write this on your handout, write the word *Entitlement*. It's sort of a comfort zone: not much asked of people."

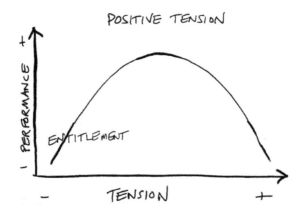

Eddie took a step back from the whiteboard and looked at each of the people in the audience. "When I say the word entitlement, what kind of thoughts come to mind?

Eileen shouted out, "You owe me something!"

"Excellent", said Eddie. "That's exactly right. People are walking around with their hands out and feeling like they don't have to earn stuff but instead feel like it is owed to them. You kind of know entitlement mentality when you see it. And it's certainly not healthy in an organiza-tion to have people walking around with their hands out expecting something for nothing. Fundamentally, entitled people believe they should get stuff because of who they are and not what they do. It's all about 'Me.'

"How did entitlement come about?" Eddie asked rhetorically. "I don't know for sure, but I have some ideas. I think, as parents, we believe self-esteem is very important for our kids. I believe it's important, and I'm sure you do as well. Somewhere along the way, we got this idea that we had to *give* self-esteem to our kids, and we started doing crazy things.

"I'll tell you about a simple example with my daughter. When she was much younger, we did the wooden derby car race together. Have you heard of that?"

Some of the members nodded.

"It's a parent/child bonding event. Anyway, we designed a wooden derby car. I carved it, she sanded and painted it, then glued on some colorful characters. It was a fun father/daughter activity. When we went to the race, there were about 40 girls competing there. We didn't win—three other girls took first, second, and third place. So, the winners are standing up there on the podium getting their trophies, and suddenly, this guy rolls out this table with 40 trophies on it.

"Every girl got a trophy! And I thought to myself, *What is going on here? What are we teaching our kids?* Next year when the race comes around, how hard is my daughter going to try if she knows she's going to get a trophy no matter what? What is this doing to her productivity? It's killing it! That's what entitlement mentality does to a person. It kills their productivity. If they know they are going to be taken care of, how hard do they really need to try?

"The truth is, we lost sight of one simple fact: you can't give self-esteem to someone. There is only one way to get self-esteem. What is it?" Eddie paused for effect.

"Earn it," said Miguel.

"Yes, you have to earn it," said Eddie. "That's how you build self-esteem. When you apply this basic concept to the workplace, it's the same thing. Bonuses and incentives should be earned compensation, not gifts. There should be a reward for a job well done. When someone gets a bonus, they should know exactly what they did to earn it. Then, they feel a sense of accomplishment, and that helps them build a feeling of self-worth. They earn their confidence. It is not given to them. This gives them a sense of purpose."

Eddie paused. He could tell he had hit a nerve with the group. They were completely tracking.

"In companies that are mired in entitlement, anxiety is low because there is not much asked of people. They are rewarded for busyness, and you hear things like: 'I have it coming,' 'I did the best I could,' and, 'I like things just the way they are.' It's a very comfortable environment, but when people are too comfortable," Eddie pointed to the bottom left of the curve again, "you see the effect on productivity.

"So, if entitlement is all about me, what's the opposite? What is the ideal? What is our purpose here? What are we trying to do through our company if we are not living in entitlement?"

There was an uncomfortable silence before Eddie continued. "Most of the companies we work with want to create great places to work. In places where the employees are engaged, they get it, are motivated, accountable, and driven, and rewarded for accomplishing results.

"As you move up the bell curve here towards this middle section, you find companies that are achievement-oriented. You'll hear things like, 'Have you thought it through?' 'Let's go for excellence,' and, 'Shoot for the big one!' These companies have a culture of enthusiasm, engagement, excitement, and celebration. There is a higher level of urgency. People are challenging each other in a positive way. There is more asked of people. This is an environment that develops better leaders; this is a place where people are learning and growing.

"There's a lot of research out there that suggests that motivation is highest when the chance of success is only 50 percent. The potential for failure is actually a motivation for people. It's ultimately quite rewarding for people because when they try something they didn't know they could do and they succeed, they build confidence. They realize the joy of accomplishment. If they fail, they learn from that, and they can do it better or differently the next time.

"So, the middle zone of the curve, I call the 'Earning' zone. Write down the word 'Earning' at the top of your bell curve, zone 2.

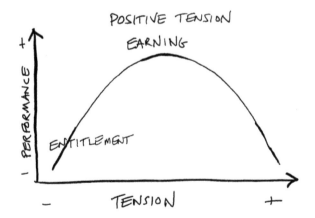

"In the Earning zone, as we said, we have this higher level of performance. What are some tools that your companies have introduced to ask more of your people, to ask more from your team?"

"We use Scorecards, like you mentioned earlier. Would those be something that adds tension?" asked Dexter.

"Scorecards are a great example," said Eddie. "How many of you use Scorecards on a regular basis?" Everyone's hands went up. "Looks like Bill has been really good at encouraging you to use measurables and Scorecards with your teams. That's great!" said Eddie.

Bill said, "We've been talking a lot about EOS in this group, and Scorecards and measurables are a big part of that, as you know, Eddie."

"Great, thanks, Bill. What's another tool that you might use to increase tension?"

"We have a set of core values that we absolutely love," said Eileen. "We hire, fire, review, reward, and recognize around core values. During the hiring process, we actually interview for core values alignment. We want to level-set expectations before anybody is invited to join Swan Services. We expect team members to behave in alignment with our 5 simple core values. I feel like that would be a great example of positive tension," she said.

Eddie said, "Eileen, that is fantastic! I wish more companies would strengthen their People Component™ by using core values like you just described. It sounds like you're already running on EOS, is that right?"

"Yes," Eileen said. "We implemented it about three years ago with an EOS Implementer, and it was a game changer for our organization."

"While we're on the EOS topic then," Eddie said, "a few other Tension Tools that fall into this category of creating higher levels of performance would be Level 10 Meetings™, To-Do Lists, Issues Lists, Rocks, starting and ending meetings on time, and there are many, many others. We've found that companies running on EOS, or really any structured operating system with its own language, have much higher levels of performance than companies that don't.

"Sometimes we refer to it as a company of ownership thinkers or an ownership culture. In this type of organization, we have a highly engaged group of people who are all striving for the same vision, and they're very comfortable challenging each other and challenging the status quo to make sure the right answer is discovered.

"In the middle of the bell curve is where a company has more tension. There's more stretch. They're setting higher expectations of performance for everyone in the company. There is more asked of everyone in the company. And the team develops an earning mindset.

"From Entitlement to Earning is where you have stated expectations around things like core values. They add pressure. All those little tools we teach in EOS add higher expectations. The right measurables on Scorecards add pressure. If you're running on EOS, you are doing these things already. It's wonderful. We're adding some stretch to create higher levels of performance.

"In organizations like this, the people are challenging each other. They're interacting with positive tension, getting to the right answers, and fighting for the greater good of the organization.

"You can use this natural law in your personal life, too. Let's say you decide to run a half marathon, and it's three months from now. What are some things you might do to prepare for that?"

Eddie waited for the group to think about it, and Dexter shouted out, "Schedule your training on a calendar!"

"Great," said Eddie. "What else?"

Jane said, "Hire a coach."

"Excellent."

"Watch your diet," John said.

"Yep. These suggestions are all types of discipline. They increase the tension in your life because, ultimately, you want to show up at that starting line and have a great race, right?

"If you don't train at all over here," Eddie said, pointing to the bottom left of the curve, "you don't have any tension in your life. If you don't do anything differently, you're not going to have an excellent performance.

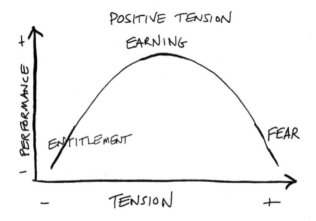

"Over here," he said, pointing to the bottom right side of the bell curve, "if you overtrain or you get injured or you overthink or you wait until the last minute, all those behaviors could cause you to underperform as well, or maybe not even show up at the starting line. You may snap.

"So, we've got entitlement here to the left, we've got earning in the middle, and over here on the right if, as leaders, we turn up the tension or pressure dial so high that performance actually decreases, what should we call that area of our bell curve?"

"Fear," Bob blurted out.

"Absolutely right, Bob," said Eddie, "That's zone 3, Fear. And in a culture of fear, people aren't worried about doing a great job. What are they worried about?"

"Self-preservation," said Miguel.

"Not getting yelled at," said Eileen.

"Yes! It's a dog-eat-dog kind of environment, and people are most interested in self-preservation rather than focusing on doing a great job," said Eddie.

"In high anxiety organizations—think about very top-down, high ego cultures—people are no longer striving for excellence. They are actually feeling so much pressure that they have sort of a fight, flight, or freeze reaction. So, performance increases and then eventually decreases in proportion to the amount of tension you exert." Eddie paused and moved to the side of the whiteboard.

"So, if you go down this path from entitlement to earning, and you start injecting accountability into the culture by asking more of people and setting higher expectations of performance, it can be scary. People can't hide because the light is shining on them. There is more expected of them. They are measured on results, and the tendency could be for people to move to fear.

"In companies that operate in fear mode," Eddie was pointing to the right side of the curve, "you'll hear these kinds of things: 'You can never let up,' 'Watch out,' and, 'Make me safe.' Because when there's fear, you can see from the graph what happens to productivity: it falls because people are consumed with anxiety. You usually find this kind of thing in a very centralized company, a top-down culture."

Martha got up to refill her coffee cup, and a few members shifted in their seats.

"As you can see and as we've discussed, there is an art, a subtle art, to being a great leader and helping your team stay at the top of this bell curve. We have to introduce, and we have to reinforce frequently and consistently, these tension tools to create these higher levels of performance. It's helpful to share this concept with your employees because it really is a natural law, sort of like gravity. You can't argue with it. Arguing with reality is fruitless.

"This is context for everything we're going to talk about today in our short time together," Eddie continued. "Let's look at a couple of other models and see how they relate to this concept," he said.

"How many have read the book *5 Dysfunctions of a Team* by Patrick Lencioni?" Eddie asked.

A few of the members raised their hands.

"Great. So, those of you who have will recognize this, but even if you haven't read the book, I am confident the concept will resonate with you. In his book, Lencioni teaches us that there are five dysfunctions he sees in teams that struggle. He calls these dysfunctions 'Trust, Conflict, Commitment, Accountability, and Results.'" Eddie returned to the board and drew a pyramid.

"When we look at the concept of conflict on teams, Lencioni teaches us that there is a continuum, starting with no conflict, which he refers to as 'artificial harmony.'" Eddie pointed to the left side of the tension axis on the whiteboard, where the word "Entitlement" was written.

"An absence of conflict is not actually a good thing! Teams that have no conflict may be sweeping issues under the rug, hoping they'll go away, and are actually ignoring problems. They may have a fear of conflict or be unwilling to discuss a problem, and that certainly doesn't allow the problem to be solved. You can see that, as a result, performance would be low.

"If you look at the opposite end of that spectrum, over here on the right," Eddie pointed to the word *Fear* on the right side of the line, "you can imagine a team that argues and fights or engages in bitter, personal attacks, or uses lots of sarcasm. Over time, they can create a culture of fear, where people are literally afraid, and that is certainly not a healthy working environment either.

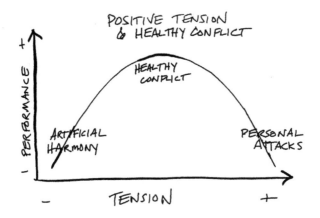

"So, what Lencioni teaches us is that some level of what he calls 'healthy conflict' leads to higher levels of performance. These teams are fighting for the greater good. They discuss real business issues, and if it gets heated, and they begin to venture down the curve this way," Eddie pointed again to fear, "they know they need to take a break or cool off or apologize. Teams like this tend to have a higher degree of emotional intelligence, so their awareness of when this is happening is more alert.

"Another book that fits this Positive Tension curve was written by a woman named Kim Scott. She wrote *Radical Candor,* in which she describes a model around management and communication. Hers is a 2x2 matrix that plots *speak directly* on the horizontal axis," Eddie pointed to the horizontal tension line, "against *care personally* on the vertical axis." He pointed to the performance axis.

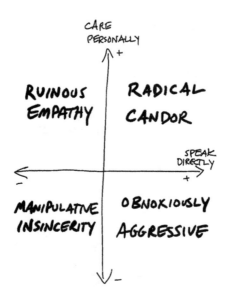

"At the top of the positive tension curve is 'radical candor,' higher levels of performance. You enter the danger, and you're open and honest, and you just say it.

"Over here on the left, she calls this 'ruinous empathy.' This occurs when you care personally but you don't speak directly. 'I'm not gonna say anything, but I care.' It's the same concept as Lencioni's artificial harmony.

"And over here on the right, this is 'obnoxiously aggressive.' 'I'm speaking directly, but I am so direct that it appears I really don't give a darn about you,' right? That type of communication style can create fear, which again lowers levels of performance.

"As you can see, a lot of thought leaders teach similar concepts but use different words. All of this can help us really understand the Positive Tension curve at a deeper level.

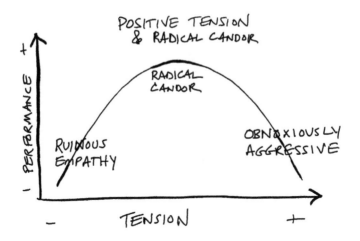

"How does that land for you guys?" Eddie asked. "Have you experienced this sort of environment before?"

Miguel shared a story about his organization from a few years earlier, where he helped his team understand that positive tension can result in exceptional productivity.

Eddie continued, "As we start to talk about incentive plans and fostering an ownership mentality among employees, I want to make one final point." Eddie pointed to the curve on the whiteboard again.

"We talked about your companies keeping score with financial statements. And sharing financial information with employees can be scary, right? Think about this, though: When you don't share anything, you keep them in the dark. You're essentially closed book."

Eddie was pointing to the left side of the curve again. "If there's nothing shared with people, they're basically living in entitlement. We have not clearly stated any expectations for them. It's actually our fault when people are living in entitlement because we haven't done a good job of clearly saying what we want and what we expect or holding people accountable. Perhaps we've just been rewarding people for showing up.

"If you open the books a bit, start sharing more information with your team, and state higher expectations of performance by saying something like, 'Use these numbers,' things will change. Employees will understand what 'gross margin' is, they'll figure out what 'net income' means, or what 'profit before tax' is, and, ultimately, how profit works for them. They will easily understand what the major lines on the income statement are.

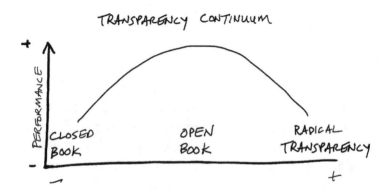

"Over here on the right, there's radical transparency, which occurs when we share too much information. Sharing salaries or sharing confidential information that could damage the company if it got out is an example of radical transparency. When people have too much information, it can be stressful. They can be paralyzed: fight, flight, or freeze. Again, when people are living in fear, productivity suffers.

"We always need to use good judgment about what we share, how much we share, with whom we share it, how often, and so forth. I'm not saying you need to open all the books," Eddie clarified, "but I do know that people make better decisions when they have good information. If you respect and trust your people, you should share some information with them. Share what you're comfortable sharing. The bottom line is, if there is something that would damage the company if it got out, don't share it."

"Are you suggesting," asked John Fredrickson, "that if I don't share financial information with my team, I don't respect them?" John was the argumentative type in the business roundtable meetings, always playing devil's advocate when Miguel, Eileen, or any of the other "bleeding edge" members proposed a new idea to the group.

"Let's have that conversation. Let's go there," said Eddie, smiling.

"Thank you," said John.

"John, I take it you're not a fan of sharing financial information with your organization?" Eddie asked.

"That's right," replied John.

"OK, can you talk a little about that? What holds you back?"

"They don't need to know that," John said emphatically. "It doesn't mean I don't respect them—they just don't need to know that."

"Do you use Scorecards and measurables?" Eddie asked.

"Of course. And we're doing just fine without sharing, so I don't see the point," John said quickly.

Eddie thought for a moment, then asked, "Can I ask a question that perhaps is more sensitive?"

"Sure."

"What are you afraid of?" Eddie asked directly. Eddie let the question hang there.

John became visibly agitated. "I'm not afraid of anything!" he exclaimed. "I just know that if I share financial information with them, they're going to want more money!"

"Aha," said Eddie. "So your fear is that if you share more information with your employees about the financial picture of your company, they're going to want more money? Is that right?"

Eddie jumped to the whiteboard and wrote *FEARS: 1) They'll want more money.*

FEARS w/ SHARING FINANCIALS:

1) THEY'LL WANT MORE MONEY

"That's right," said John. "I wouldn't call it a fear; it's just reality."

"OK, I get it," said Eddie. "What else?"

"If we share financial information with the employees," said John, "they're going to think that I'm taking home way more than I really am."

"Alright, what's the problem with that?" asked Eddie.

"Well, it builds up animosity, I suppose. There's a wall between us and them. It's a fairness issue. It'll create division in the company," John responded.

Eddie wrote *2) Thinking I'm making wheelbarrows of money (if good news)* on the whiteboard.

FEARS w/ SHARING FINANCIALS:

1) THEY'LL WANT MORE MONEY

2) THEY'LL THINK I'M MAKING
   WHEELBARROWS FULL OF MONEY

"This is good stuff," said Eddie. "What else? Anyone—what else are we afraid will happen if we share financial information with our employees?"

"Well, if we share bad news," said Miguel, "we may be afraid that everyone will run for the door."

"Great answer," said Eddie. "So if we share good news, people think we're making wheelbarrows full of money, and if we share bad news, people are gonna quit because they think we're going out of business? Is that right?" Eddie asked.

"Exactly," said John.

Eddie wrote down *3) They'll flee (if bad news)*.

FEARS w/ SHARING FINANCIALS:

1) THEY'LL WANT MORE MONEY

2) THEY'LL THINK I'M MAKING
   WHEELBARROWS FULL OF MONEY

3) THEY'LL FLEE IF BAD NEWS

"Now, I'm not going to try to dispel these stories right now, necessarily," said Eddie, "but I will tell you that this is the same list of three items I've heard for 27 years. In my experience, these are 'stories.' These are things that we tell ourselves over and over again. Because we're afraid of making a change, we believe the stories in our heads, and the irony is we believe that these are the stories in our employees' heads, too.

"In the absence of information, people make up their own stories, right? So, you do have a choice when it comes to sharing information: You can certainly not share any information, and then you have to deal with the consequences of the story that people will make up in their heads, whether it's that you're making tons of money, or it's not fair, or whatever the story in their head may be.

"Or, you can share some information, again, whatever level of transparency you're comfortable with, and you get to create the story that's in their head. In my experience, employees have the capacity and the interest to understand this stuff. We'll talk about how to do that later this morning. Let's leave these three fears here on the whiteboard as we get into the ProfitWorks Solution, then revisit them when we talk about the third element: the Missing Link™.

PSYCHOLOGICAL SAFETY

"Before we break, one last point on this. Let's say you've got people living over here in entitlement: maybe not your entire organization, but some people. The folks in your organization may be sprinkled all along this bell curve, and certainly, we want everybody at the top of the bell curve whenever possible. But let's say you do have some people over here on the left, where it's pretty comfortable. It's a comfort zone for them, and there's not much asked of them, like we said. Then you start introducing Tension Tools like Scorecards, measurables, and some of the other examples we talked about. These people might have sort of a deer-in-the-headlights look, right? Where do you think the first place they're going to run to on this bell curve is when more is asked of them, and you're kind of moving their cheese?"

"Fear," Bob blurted it out again.

"That's right. You're kind of obsessed with fear today, aren't you, Bob?" Eddie joked.

Everyone laughed.

"I'm just teasing you. But you're exactly right, Bob. When people feel pressure, the first place they tend to run is to the right side of the positive tension curve. They're thinking, 'I can't hide anymore.' Let's talk about how we avoid that.

"We just talked a little about Lencioni's Five Dysfunctions model." Eddie drew the simple pyramid with five levels on the whiteboard. "This trust pyramid is nothing new to you. You can see we have Vulnerability-Based Trust at the foundation, and going up the pyramid, from there we have Conflict . . ." Eddie was labeling the levels as he was teaching: *Commitment, Accountability,* and *Results*.

"After ten years as an EOS Implementer, my experience is that when you have really strong core values, and you do as Eileen suggested: hiring, reviewing, and reinforcing within your organization on a regular formal basis around core values, you create an organization where vulnerability-based trust is very strong.

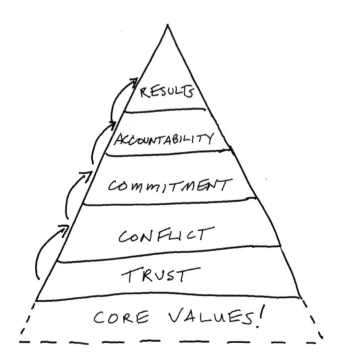

"So, our core values truly become the foundation of Lencioni's pyramid. Our core values are a behavioral agreement that we have that we're going to treat each other like adults. With that in mind, the Adult Agreement™ is basically a verbal handshake between you and your workforce that says, 'Because we're all adults here, and we all want basically the same things from working here: a great place to work, an enjoyable environment, and financial opportunities, we agree to do certain things, and we agree *not* to do certain things.'

"For example, we agree that we will live and breathe our core values. We have mutual respect. We help each other. We take care of each other. We believe in healthy conflict. We can disagree and commit. We don't ignore problems. We put issues on the issues list. We're going to talk about it. We're going to enter the danger. We create clarity and buy-in. We hold each other accountable. And we fight for the greater good. Right up Lencioni's pyramid." Eddie pointed to *Results*.

"We also create psychological safety," he continued. "This is a concept that is becoming more current as more research is done on team dynamics, but psychological safety is critical for healthy teams. It's defined as a 'shared belief held by members of a team that the group is a safe place for taking risks.'

"Adults also trust each other, and we don't attack each other. As Lencioni says, mean-spirited personal attacks create fear. From the Positive Tension curve, we know that fear creates lower levels of performance."

Eddie took several minutes to write an Adult Agreement on the whiteboard.

ADULT AGREEMENT

ADULTS DO:

- LIVE OUR CORE VALUES
- CREATE PSYCHOLOGICAL SAFETY
- HAVE HEALTHY CONFLICT
- FIGHT FOR THE GREATER GOOD

ADULTS DON'T:

- ATTACK EACH OTHER
- SHOOT THE MESSENGER
- IGNORE PROBLEMS
- DISRESPECT EACH OTHER

"Also, we don't shoot the messenger. As an example, let's say we work in an environment where people are known to shoot the messenger, and I have an idea. We try it out, and it doesn't work. If I get shot for that, what's going to happen the next time I have an idea?" Eddie asked the group.

"You won't say it," Miguel replied.

"Right. I'll disregard it," said Eddie, "and that's not a healthy environment.

"Or, let's say I make a mistake and own up to it. If I get yelled at for that, what's going to happen the next time I make a mistake?"

"You'll hide it," said Julia.

"I'll hide it for fear of being shot down," said Eddie. "When we have a psychologically safe environment, we don't hide problems.

"Another thing adults do is acknowledge reality. 'It is what it is.' We can't go back and change that. What we can do is learn from our mistakes and grow from them, but we can't argue with reality. It gets us nowhere.

"Adults also respect each other. We take care of each other. We protect each other, and we protect the company. By that, I mean if we're going to start sharing more information about the company with everyone, perhaps confidential information, we don't share that outside the company. We don't want our competitors or our customers getting their hands on it. As we said, if there really is something that would be damaging if it got out, there's an easy solution to that: Don't share it!

"So, psychological safety is an important precursor for being successful with what we'll talk about today. Pretty simple stuff, but quite profound. This sense of safety helps people attack the problems and not the personalities. You get a lot more accomplished because people are focused on the business issues, and all their arrows are pointed in the same direction; they're acting professionally, and it takes the emotion out of it.

"So that's the Adult Agreement. Steal like an artist!" said Eddie. "Many of my clients print it out and laminate it and put it up in the lunchroom or whatever, where people can see it frequently and be reminded. It works nicely with Lencioni's pyramid, and it helps you stay in the Earning zone up here. As leaders, we have to model it.

"This agreement really requires that the leaders go first. We must model this—we must *be the message*, as leadership author Warren Bennis says. We have to walk the talk and show them. We are the message, so we must hold up our part of the Adult Agreement. This type of integrity creates such a healthy foundation for staying at the top of the bell curve for longer periods of time," Eddie continued. "Recognizing that there are no perfect human beings, of course, I don't know that it's possible to stay at the top of the bell curve 100 percent of the time, but if we're there 80 to 90 percent of the time, we've got a super organization, a company of excellence, rather than just pockets of excellence here and there in the company."

Eileen loved the setup and felt like Eddie was talking to her.

Eddie finished up. "Let's take a break, and then we'll do a group activity."

CHAPTER 4

THE PROFITWORKS SOLUTION

After the group returned from the break and settled back in their seats, Eddie continued, "How is this landing for you? What are your initial thoughts and reflections?"

After some discussion, Eddie said, "These concepts are the context for everything we're going to talk about while we're together. Over the several decades we've been doing this work, it has developed into this model called the ProfitWorks Solution.

"The ProfitWorks Solution has three elements to it. The first one is called the organizational operating system. This is about getting really strong with your leadership team on three things: a clear vision, execution, which includes discipline and accountability, and a healthy culture. Although we won't go into too much detail on the operating system today, we will talk about it first because that's really the locomotive. That's where everything has to start: with the leadership team.

"The second element we're going to talk about is called the No-Entitlement Incentive Plan. This is about creating an incentive plan that moves everyone in your organization into an earning mindset. An effective incentive plan can help teams move away from an entitlement mentality and toward an earning mentality.

"The third and final element we'll talk about—we'll actually spend quite a bit of time on it today—is called the Missing Link. This is about building an ownership culture. It's about making it all come to life. If we're going to have an incentive plan based on profitability, we have to do the hard work of educating everyone about what drives profitability in your organization, and tie all the Tension Tools that you have today, then introduce several others to help everyone become active participants in finding the money to fund their incentive plan. I say *'their* incentive plan' because, ideally, this is not a bonus that you're giving them as a gift at the end of the year. It's actually an earned compensation plan. It's in their power to find the dollars to fund the incentive plan through their changed behavior," Eddie explained.

"So, that's the model at a high level, and my plan today is to go deep into each of these three elements with you, share some ideas and some stories with you, and ask you for your ideas and stories as well. Ideally, all of us will leave here with a clear understanding of the simplicity of the ProfitWorks Solution. Sound like a good plan?" he asked.

ORGANIZATIONAL OPERATING SYSTEM

Everyone nodded their yeses, so Eddie moved on and said, "Let's talk about an organizational operating system. As I mentioned earlier, I'm an EOS Implementer and have been for over ten years. Show of hands, how many have heard of the book *Traction* by Gino Wickman?"

Everyone raised their hands.

"Great," said Eddie, "and how many of you are actually running on EOS, whether you're self-implementing or you've hired an implementer, like Eileen did?"

More than half the group raised their hands. "Good, good. That gives me some good information because this talk isn't about EOS specifically. I just want to make a few key points here. When we get into talking about the incentive plan, one of the most critical points to understand is that the incentive plan is not going to manage your people. Your leaders and managers still have to do that heavy lifting.

"That was my discovery about ten years ago. I had been doing all this work to try to help companies build a higher level of employee engagement in their businesses, help them get aligned, and teach them to think and act like owners. In reality, most of the leadership teams with whom I was working were not aligned with the vision themselves. We were essentially trying to engage employees in an undeclared, and certainly unshared, vision," Eddie explained.

"The short story is that if we do the hard work of getting up and running on an operating system—we'll focus today on EOS—then your company will get better at three things: Vision, Traction®, and Healthy.

"Vision describes an environment where you and your leadership team are 100 percent on the same page with who you are, where you're going, and how you're going to get there. Traction helps you create accountability and discipline in your organization to help you achieve that vision. 'Healthy' means creating a healthy, functional, cohesive leadership team because most leadership teams are not. And as goes the leadership team, so goes the rest of the organization.

"You'll actually get to a point where everyone in your organization is 100 percent in alignment and sharing that vision, everyone is operating with discipline and accountability to help you execute toward that vision, and everyone in the organization is behaving in a way that is healthy, functional, and cohesive. It's really powerful!" Eddie exclaimed.

"Eileen, Miguel, can you talk a little about your experience with EOS?" he asked.

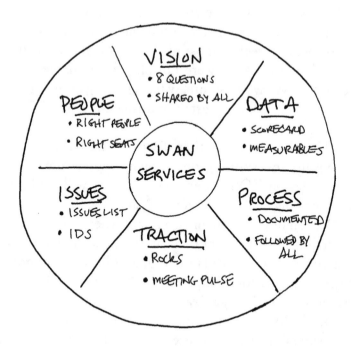

Image used with permission.

Eileen and Miguel shared a little about their experience with their Implementer, Alan, the EOS Model, the EOS Toolbox™, and the EOS Process®. Eddie thanked them and continued.

"I won't go through each of these Six Key Components™ of your business in detail today, but I strongly encourage you, if this is resonating with you, or if Eileen's and Miguel's strong testimonial is any indication, please read *Traction*.

RIGHT PEOPLE, RIGHT SEATS

"Diving just a little deeper into the People Component, we've all heard the Jim Collins mantra that we must have the right people in the right seats, right?"

Everyone nodded.

"Having the Right People on board is critical to creating a company of excellence. If you don't have the right people, you'll soon find that you have pockets of excellence. We don't want pockets of excellence; we want everyone to be firing on all cylinders all the time. That's the way the best companies do that hard work. Let me touch on this for a moment, but I won't dwell on it.

"We talked earlier about the fact that what creates financial performance in a company is the people. No matter what the company or industry, it's always about two things: the people in the business and all the stuff they do. Having the right people is critical.

"Now, we've all heard the phrase 'Hire Slowly and Fire Quickly,' but I have to say, most companies do the exact opposite. They hire quickly and fire slowly, and that is exactly the wrong way to do it. When we don't take our time to find the right person for the job, we make errors. That leads to turnover, which is very expensive. We want to take our time and make sure we fully vet our new hires.

"The same goes for firing," Eddie went on. "If we don't fire quickly or hang on to poor performers who we realize are not coachable or productive or ethical, or whatever, it really becomes a credibility issue.

"Think about it this way: let's say you have a poor performer on your team, and everyone knows it. This person is not pulling their weight. They are actually a drag on the company. Months go by with no change. When you finally let that person go, what's everyone else usually thinking?"

"What took you so long?" said Amy.

"Finally," said John.

"Exactly," said Eddie, "and it damages your credibility if you hang on to poor performers for too long, not to mention the damage it can do to morale and productivity in the organization. Now, that being said, you need to make sure you go through your people process, but we don't want to hang on to dead weight.

"Another point about having the Right People is that often when companies go down this path to build a culture of accountability, there are some employees who don't want to pull their weight. What kind of employees don't want to pull their weight?"

"Deadweight," said Jane.

"Right. Typically, poor performers don't want to pull their weight. For a company that chooses to do business this way, it can become a self-selecting process. You may have employees holding *each other* accountable, and they don't tolerate poor performance for very long, especially if it is impacting their incentive and their work environment. Many times, those poor performers get pushed out or decide for themselves that 'This is not the place for me. I'll go work somewhere else.' They separate from the company, and you know what? That's just fine. Again, we want a company of excellence, and it takes great people to create that.

"The last thing I'll say about the Right People revolves around a statistic. According to the National Center for Employee Ownership, companies that do business this way—with an engaged workforce and a culture of excellence—retain employees at a 200 percent better rate than companies that don't. People really enjoy working in companies with a culture of excellence and engagement;

they don't want to leave. Employees are challenged, they are growing both personally and professionally, they are rewarded both intrinsically and extrinsically—or financially—and it simply becomes part of who they are. The cultural fit is there, and it feels great.

"When you look at all the reasons why people leave companies, it's the non-financial reasons that really drive them out: 'I don't like my boss;' 'I'm not growing;' 'I'm not challenged,' and so forth. They may say it's the money, but surveys tell us otherwise. It's easier to say it's the money than it is to talk about the real reasons.

"Those two disciplines, Right People and Right Seats, are the ones that strengthen the People Component. There are a lot of other tools in the EOS Toolbox that will help you do that, too.

"But let's come back to the incentive plan. You can see it becomes pretty clear that we don't want to develop an incentive plan and pay out incentive plan dollars to people if they're really not the right people or if they're not in the right seat. Right?" Eddie asked.

"So we have to do that hard people work first. If you have a great culture with 100 percent of the right people in the right seats, that's fantastic, and the rest of this talk should really resonate with you. But if you don't, it doesn't mean it won't work, it just means it's a bit of a longer journey," Eddie explained.

PERFORMANCE VALUES MATRIX

"Next, I want to share a tool called the performance values matrix. This is one I stumbled upon through reading about Jack Welch, the famous former CEO at GE. It simplifies the way you think about people in your organization. As you can see, I'm a big fan of the X-axis and the Y-axis," Eddie grinned. He finished drawing another 2x2 matrix on the whiteboard.

"You can see on the X axis here—the horizontal bar— we have performance from low to high, and on the Y axis, we have core values from low to high. A simple way to imagine the right person being in the right seat is this: this person is living and breathing your core values, you absolutely love them, you wish you could clone them, they knock it out of the park with their performance, they really own their role, they hit all their measurables, and they follow the core processes. This is an RPRS, a Right Person Right Seat. This goes in the upper right-hand corner of our grid. I call these folks rock stars or superstars." Eddie wrote the word Stars and wrote RPRS underneath it.

"Ideally, you want everybody in your organization to be somewhere up in this upper right quadrant, but sometimes you can't hire superstars, you can't hire rock stars. Maybe they're too expensive, or you just can't find them, so you agree to hire somebody who's definitely core-values-aligned, like Eileen said. She hires for core values.

"But perhaps they don't quite yet have the performance you're striving for. I call employees who aren't quite there *yet* Puppies. And what do you do with puppies?"

"You train them," said Bob.

"That's right," said Eddie, "and if puppies aren't behaving or they poop on the floor or something, metaphorically, of course, what do you do?"

"You whack them with a newspaper?" offered Bill.

Everyone laughed.

As the laughter subsided, Eddie said, "Well, you certainly help them learn from that, right? Maybe we say, 'You clean up their messes.' So that's a right person in the wrong seat, and hopefully, it's just temporary. If they gain the capacity, ideally, they will move into the upper right quadrant with our rock stars."

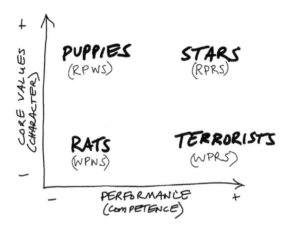

Eddie wrote the word puppies in the upper left quadrant and wrote RPWS below it.

"Now, over here on the bottom left, we have somebody who is not core-values-aligned. They refuse to behave in alignment with the stated expectations of your unique core values, and they are also underperformers. They aren't good at their jobs, and they don't hit their numbers. Those are called WPWS, wrong person/wrong seat people."

Eddie wrote WPWS and wrote the word 'Rats' in the bottom left quadrant.

"I use the term 'Rats,' and the only reason for that is it's the word 'star' spelled backward. They're 180 degrees from what we want. But if you think about rats on a boat, when you shine the light on them, and you're measuring performance, and you have Scorecards, and you have high expectations of performance, a lot of times rats run for the shadows. Ideally, they jump overboard. A lot of times, though, you have to help hoist them over the edge. You try to train them, you coach them, and you shine the light on the behavioral 'data points' as we call them in EOS. Most of us are pretty good at identifying and taking care of wrong person/wrong seat issues.

"The toughest ones to handle are here in the bottom right, I've found." Eddie wrote the word "Terrorists."

"These people are wrong people; they don't share your core values, but they're in the right seat. They're very good at what they do, they're hitting all their numbers, and they kind of fool you. And you're thinking, 'Oh, we can't fire that guy, he's hitting all his numbers! He's our star sales guy!' But you've noticed that they're incredibly toxic in your organization. They can almost be like a cancer in the organization. They are WPRS," he said while writing the letters below.

"Here's a question for you: if you hang onto your terrorist for too long, what do you think your stars are eventually going to do?" Eddie asked.

"They'll leave," Dexter sheepishly commented.

"That's right!" Eddie confirmed. "Usually, stars know that they're pretty good, and if they have to deal with terrorists day in and day out, they're going to be pretty open to finding another organization, one where there's zero tolerance for that kind of behavior. So, 'your stars will go out' if you hang on to terrorists for too long.

"The other thing that terrorists do in organizations is they recruit puppies. They pull them into their sinister little world and try to create a tribe of what author Dave Logan calls Level 1 or Level 2 organizations. People like this teach others that 'Life sucks,' or 'My Life Sucks,' as he says in his book *Tribal Leadership*.

"So, you have a choice. As we get into incentive plans and discuss some of the details and mechanics of those, I want to be sure to level-set your expectations. If you have people issues, an incentive plan isn't going to solve those issues. You need to do the hard work of hiring and firing around core values and performance.

"One additional point that's really powerful, as it relates to this performance values matrix, comes from Stephen M.R. Covey and a book called *The Speed of Trust*. In his work, he teaches us that Character and Competence are the foundation for high-trust relationships. Different words, same concept. Character is equivalent to core values. It's who you are at your core: your integrity and your behavior define your character.

"Competence is essentially your capacity and your skill, or how good you are at your job. This would be our performance continuum along the X-axis.

"Ultimately, when we talk about the ProfitWorks Solution, we mean building a high-trust culture where everyone in your organization is thinking and acting like an owner. We are striving for 100 percent right person right seats, and we have the tools and discipline to do that.

FROM ME TO WE

"My background has given me a very holistic view of how businesses work," Eddie continued. "I look at businesses from a financial perspective, and it is clear to me that when you boil it all down, business is about making money. If we don't do that, we won't be able to do anything else, including cultivating a productive, healthy culture. And I also look at businesses from the people side, so I know that it's possible to be very financially focused in a very high involvement, high engagement, transparent environment. It's a very healthy way to run a business! This is what ProfitWorks is all about: it's about being Healthy and Smart.

"Let's talk about what ProfitWorks means conceptually. To do that, I'd like each of you to put on your owner's hat. Most of you are owners of your business. What do owners think about? What keeps you awake at night?" he asked the group. They rattled off answers:

"Cash."

"Paying the bills, costs."

"The economy."

"Profit."

"Employees."

"New business, growth."

"Excellent," said Eddie.

Eddie had drawn two columns on the whiteboard, and in the left-hand column, titled *Owner*, he was writing their responses.

He continued, "Now, I want you to take your owner's hat off for a minute and put on the hat of a typical employee. What do most employees think about? What do they worry about?"

"Their paycheck," offered Bob. The others followed with answers.

"Benefits."

"Doing a good job."

"The boss."

"The culture," said Jane.

"Job security."

"Getting a raise."

Eddie was writing on the list in the second column; he titled it *Employee*.

"Work Environment: is this a good place to work?"

"Opportunity to grow."

OWNER	EMPLOYEE
CASH	PAYCHECK
GROWTH	BENEFITS
PEOPLE	JOB SECURITY
ECONOMY	WORK ENVIRONMENT
COSTS	FRIDAY
PROFIT	OPPORTUNITIES

WE ⟵⟶ ME

"Great," said Eddie. "When you look at this list on the right, the Employee list, what is this list about?" Eddie asked, pointing to the employee list.

"Me," said John, "the employee."

"Right, it's about 'Me,'" said Eddie, "and what is this list about over here?" he asked, pointing to the *Owner* side.

"It's about the company," said Julia.

"Yes, it's about the company. So, conceptually, this is what ProfitWorks is all about. Moving from 'Me' to 'We.' It's about helping employees think *not only* about Me, because Me is very important, but also about the company, about We. The truth is, if we take better care of the company, we can absolutely take better care of ourselves . . . through our incentive plan, through professional development at the company, better benefits, investments, opportunities to move up in the organization, and so forth."

Eddie drew a double-headed arrow connecting the two lists. "This is what creating an ownership culture is all about. It's helping employees think not only about the *Me* stuff, like this list on the right but also about the company. The truth is, and your employees will undoubtedly agree with this, the better we take care of the company through improved cash flow, more revenue growth, controlling costs, increasing operational efficiencies, and so forth, the better we can take care of ourselves. It's really about putting the greater good of the organization first. If we prioritize *We*, we can take better care of *Me*.

"It's important that we help all employees understand that profit, the engine of growth in any organization, works for everyone. If you think about the alternative, it becomes even clearer. If our revenues are shrinking, our costs are expanding, we have poor cash flow, or if some or all of the things on the left are at risk, all the things on the right are certainly going to be affected. Paychecks are at risk, benefits certainly won't expand, and job security is at risk. Without growth, there are certainly fewer opportunities, and so forth. So, the game is to help our employees see the business through the eyes of an owner: to help them think and act like owners. When we do this, we create this ownership culture where everyone sees the business with new eyes.

"In my experience, employees have the capacity and the interest to understand this stuff. When you look across all companies in all industries, a significant percentage of profits are just falling through the cracks. But do people get up in the morning and say, 'I'm going to go do a crappy job today!'? Of course not! They just aren't always engaged and don't know where to look to find the money falling through the cracks.

"So, we have to create an environment where they understand why they should care and provide them with the tools to become engaged so they can find money falling through the cracks and become active participants in funding their incentive plans. In doing so, they help drive improved financial performance at the company as well. This creates a better life for everyone—individuals and companies."

Eddie paused while the group took in the concept of Profit Works. "What are your thoughts on all of this?" he asked.

Dexter said, "I don't think my employees would be able to understand stuff like P&L statements and so forth. I've got a bunch of front-line people and they just don't have the capacity to be able to understand that."

"Okay," said Eddie. "Anybody have some thoughts or ideas for Dexter?"

Eileen said, "I can see your point, Dexter. But in my experience at Swan Services, the employees want to know what's going on. I had a conversation yesterday with an employee who thought that Vic and I were taking home the gross profit dollars."

Everyone laughed nervously.

"Can you imagine?" asked Eileen.

"Well, you've got more of a white-collar team at Swan, Eileen," said Dexter.

Miguel said, "In my experience, everyone can understand this stuff. I have a mix of front-line team members as well as people with advanced degrees, and because we are committed to sharing information as a part of the way we do business, it sinks in. For some people, it just takes longer than for others. For us, it's been about the consistency of our communication."

Eddie chimed in. "I will share with you, and Miguel, you may have seen this in your company as well: in my experience, most employees think profitability is about 30 to 50 percent of sales. Now, that's not because they're dumb," said Eddie. "It's because we haven't taught them. It's not like you go through school and take Business Literacy 101. Most people just kind of go through school, maybe some go to college, and then they get a job. If they're lucky enough to join a company that does training around this, they begin to realize that bottom line profitability is more in the range of 5 to 10 percent, and it tends to be very industry specific."

Eddie asked, "If you have employees walking around thinking that you make 50 percent profit, what's the problem with that?"

"Like John said earlier, if they think we're making 50 percent profit, they're gonna want more money," said Dexter.

"Exactly," said Eddie. "And if you start sharing a little bit of information with them to help them understand that it's not 50 percent—it's more like 10 percent—and that's before taxes, they're typically not thinking you should be giving them more money. Most likely, they will think, 'Oh my gosh, that's really tight. How do we increase that?'

"I've also seen employees increase their respect for the amount of risk that owners take when they start and run a business. There's not a lot of room for error. Why do people take risks?"

"To get a return," said Dexter.

"Absolutely," said Eddie. "And the truth is, all returns, whether it's return on sales, return on equity, return on investment, or return on inventory—all those returns come from profit. Profit is the engine of growth in a market economy. It is precious. In my experience, the companies that help their employees understand this perform at a much higher level than the companies that keep their employees in the dark.

WHAT YOUR EMPLOYEES DON'T KNOW CAN HURT YOU.

"So, as a business owner, you have a choice. You can share some information with your employees—information they're really going to care about—to try to create a stronger link between their daily activities and the company's financial performance, or you can keep them in the dark. There are consequences either way. But you have a choice as the owner."

Eddie continued. "As we said earlier, one way, you get to create the story that's in their head, and the other way, you have to live with the story they create in their head."

INFORMATION IS TENSION!

Eddie drew another horizontal line on the whiteboard. "I mentioned this before, about the continuum with transparency. Recall that on the left side of this line is 'Closed Book.' This is when you don't share any information with the organization. You might share a little bit with the leadership team, but essentially, you're a closed book.

"The middle part of the line is 'Open Book,' when you share an appropriate amount of information with the right people. You might be sharing activity-based measurables with frontline employees; you might have Scorecards and measurables visible and available to people, perhaps on a flat screen or a whiteboard in the plant, things like errors, rework, picking accuracy, labor efficiency, overtime—information that relates to the stuff they do every day.

"And the far right of the continuum is 'Radical Transparency.' Again, I don't see a lot of this, but in organizations where too much information is shared—people's salaries or confidential information about what's going on with certain people in the organization, or confidential financial information—it's just too much.

TRANSPARENCY CONTINUUM

CLOSED BOOK   OPEN BOOK   RADICAL TRANSPARENCY

"Recall our Positive Tension curve," Eddie said. "This continuum I'm showing you reveals that 'Information' is a form of tension or pressure. Providing information to employees is asking more from them. Providing information creates higher expectations of performance. When you provide information, you expect people to use that information to improve the organization. It's essentially a handshake; it's an agreement saying that if I provide more information about the company's performance, then you will use that information to improve the organization.

"And so, in this way," Eddie drew the bell curve again, "you can see that open book companies perform at a higher level. People in these companies use the information they're given to make better decisions for the company.

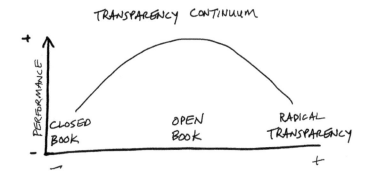

"Information is positive tension. It stretches people. Transparency is positive tension. And providing information also improves trust. Why would this be true?" he asked the group.

Eileen thought for a moment and said, "It seems like when you share information with people, you're being vulnerable. You're saying, 'This is how the game works. This is how our company keeps score.' When people receive that information," Eileen continued, "there's a subconscious feeling of being included, of being respected. It's kind of like saying I know you can understand this. You just didn't have the information before. So you're bringing people into that ownership world, as you said, Eddie."

"Wow," said Eddie, "that's great, Eileen. You're exactly right."

SCARF

Eddie continued. "One final point on this. David Rock wrote an article called "Managing with the Brain in Mind," in which he introduces a model called SCARF. In his research, he discovered that when any of five qualities are threatened, people retreat to sort of the 'lizard brain.'"

Everyone laughed.

"S stands for status, C stands for certainty, A stands for autonomy, R stands for relatedness, and F stands for fairness. When any of these five states are increased or positively affected, people move toward them with openness, sort of a reward response. As a result, chemicals like oxytocin and dopamine flow in their brains. In fact, another author, Paul Zak, calls oxytocin the 'trust chemical.'

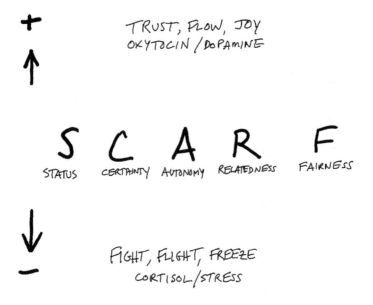

"According to Rock, when any of these five states are threatened or negatively affected, people move away from them and retreat, and chemicals like cortisol course through their systems.

"If you remember back to the Positive Tension curve," Eddie pointed to the curve on the whiteboard, "threatening any of these five things puts people in a state of fear, where they are less productive, and their lizard brain is thinking of fight, flight, or freeze. They are overwhelmed.

"When all of these five senses are supported, however, people are at the top of the bell curve. Oftentimes, they can be in a flow state, as Mihaly Csikszentmihalyi and Stephen Kotler discuss in their research on the concept of flow."

The team was nodding; Bill had just shared the same information a few months earlier after a speaker on the concept of "Flow" had spoken to the group.

"That's when people do their best work, when they are challenged, and they're slightly outside of their comfort zone because the challenge is slightly tougher than the skills they bring to the challenge; when they're stretching, but not snapping," Eddie explained.

"These concepts all relate to the idea of transparency in your organization. Transparency creates trust, the base of Lencioni's pyramid. If we want to create a high-trust culture where we're okay with healthy conflict and we resolve all the issues we debate and discuss, we need to help people understand, at a very simple level, how we keep score within the organization. That way, they can actively participate in playing the game with you, alongside you, and help you and your teams win the game. That's the result of helping your employees move from Me to We: an Ownership Culture," Eddie concluded.

CHAPTER 5

SIMPLE & SELF-FUNDED

After another break, Eddie gathered the group again and went on. "The second element of the ProfitWorks Solution that I'd like to jump into now is called The No-Entitlement Incentive Plan. This section of the talk is typically pretty interesting for members because, in my experience, everyone struggles with the concept of incentive compensation. I suppose the first reason for that is that there's not really one right answer. There is no silver bullet.

"Most incentive plans don't work," Eddie continued. "In fact, many actually damage the company. There are two primary reasons for this: one, the plans are too complicated. I think an owner gets it in their head, 'If I just design the right incentive plan, it'll manage my people.' Then they say, 'Well, these people do these things over here in operations, so I'll set up a plan for them. These people in admin do this other stuff, so we'll have a different plan for them, and pretty soon, we have a complicated system set up. Not to mention, it's really difficult to administer all these plans! When something is complicated, employees don't understand it, and if they don't understand it, they don't trust it. Also, they can't take action to improve it if they don't understand it. So, when an incentive plan is too complicated, it's a big problem.

"The second problem I see is that we design these plans and base them on some financial calculation, like gross margin or profit, but we don't bother to give our employees all the tools and training they need to understand these terms. We don't teach them business literacy, and we don't have measurables or Scorecards or Challenge Rocks or Level 10 Meetings or culture committees, or any of the other things we've been talking about. Here's what can happen in that scenario: Let's say you've got a plan that pays out quarterly. You go through the first quarter, and everyone gets a big payout. How do they feel—they just got a big bonus check?"

"Great!" Dexter said.

"That's right, it feels great! It's like getting a gift. The same thing happens the next quarter, and the next, and so on. But let's stop for a minute and talk about the purpose of an incentive plan. What should the purpose of an incentive plan be?" Eddie asked the group.

There was a brief silence. Then Martha spoke up, "To reward employees."

"OK. What else?" Eddie prompted.

"To motivate employees," said Fred.

"Good, right! Any other thoughts come to mind as we think about the purpose of an incentive plan?"

Jane spoke up. "To attract and retain employees," she said.

"Excellent," said Eddie. "Here's my definition of an effective incentive plan: an effective incentive plan should direct employees' energy toward improving the financial performance of the company. What we're talking about is psychology—human psychology—and trying to direct employee behavior so that all the arrows in the organization are pointing in the same direction." Then Eddie asked, "Is that plan I was describing directing employees' energy toward improvement?"

Most of the group shook their heads.

"No, of course not. It's actually not an incentive plan; it's an entitlement plan because the employees get used to getting this bonus. I've seen plenty of cases where employees have spent the bonus before they've even gotten it because they are so used to getting it."

Eileen closed her eyes, rubbing her forehead, thinking about Kevin's comments earlier in the week.

Eddie continued, "What inevitably happens is eventually, the company is going to get to a quarter where they have poor business performance, and there is no payout. Now, the employees don't know the company has had poor performance because no one has shared information with them. What the employees do know is they didn't get their bonus. So, what are they thinking then?"

"The owners took it," John piped up.

"Right—the owners took it. They're thinking, 'I'm doing the same stuff I was always doing, and I was always getting the bonus before. They must be screwing me.' And that's the eventual demise of most bonus plans. It can be kind of sad as an owner. I mean, you put this plan in place to be nice and to motivate and reward employees, and now everyone's pissed off at you.

"Now, for those of you who are running on EOS, you use a simple tool called the V/TO to establish agreement around a company vision: first among the leadership team, and ultimately among the entire organization. This is an agreement about who you are, what you do, where you're going, and so forth."

Eddie continued, "In order to get that vision shared by everybody in the organization, we need to provide them with a little foundational knowledge that helps them understand that we need them to actively participate in driving improvement in their areas. This type of alignment will help you achieve the vision stated on that V/TO. When you achieve this, employees also win through the payout opportunities in their incentive plan.

"The great thing about an incentive plan is that it will do all those things we listed earlier: it will motivate, reward, and help attract and retain people. If we do it just right, an incentive plan can also open their eyes to seeing the business from an owner's perspective. They'll understand that when we take better care of the *We* stuff, like what's on the V/TO, we can absolutely take better care of the *Me* stuff, like job security, opportunities for growth, raises, investment in technology and new equipment, and through incentive payouts.

"As we know, everyone appreciates a little extra something, and if we can effectively tie that extra something—the incentive pool—to their behavior, we help them understand that it has been *earned*. It's not an entitlement that you get for just showing up. 'But,' we tell them, 'you've got to actively participate as a member of the organization and see the business through the owner's eyes. Employees, we want you to share opportunities for increasing operational efficiencies, documenting processes, and improving communication between departments as one team with one voice. When we do that, when we take better care of the organization as a team, as one tribe, if you will, then we win together, and we can all share in that celebration at the end of the day.'

"So, the incentive plan isn't necessarily just dollars to be paid out to everybody on the team when we win. It is also a mechanism for creating improved trust in the organization—a culture that celebrates together and is proud of its accomplishments. In this way, the incentive plan can become a symbol of camaraderie and success. It becomes a symbol of winning, a celebration. So, we truly are playing a game together with our employees. It's not us versus them. It's all of us together.

"In this way, profit is kind of the score at the end of the game. And if we don't share any information about the score or how we're doing during the game, perhaps quarterly, it's almost like bowling with a blindfold. You throw that first ball down the lane, but you don't know how you did. It's not a lot of fun, and you don't know where to focus your next effort."

Eddie continued, "To bring it back to our incentive plan, we can all agree that the purpose of an incentive plan is to direct and manage human energy and that the impact of an incentive plan that pays out is more than just motivation and reward; it's an opportunity to help employees feel a sense of ownership. As we continue to reinforce for the employees—in a simple way—how the company makes money and how they can impact that, they begin to make efforts to take better care of the company. They begin to see when we take better care of the *We*, they'll be able to take better care of the *Me*."

Eddie went on. "When we get into the Missing Link component of the ProfitWorks Solution, we'll see that there are some simple business literacy exercises that you can teach to your employees that don't require them to be accountants, that won't require them to read detailed financial statements and become mathematicians. There are ways to teach this that help the employees understand, at a simple level initially, that business finance is not that much different from household finance.

"In my research over the last few decades, I've seen a pattern of mistakes that people make when designing incentive plans. In fact, I've made all of them myself!" said Eddie. "I'd like you to consider your experience with incentive plans and which of these mistakes perhaps you might have made.

"The first mistake I see, and we mentioned this earlier, but it's worth repeating, is that as owners, we tend to overcomplicate the formula. We make these incentive plans way too complex. If we're trying to reach all employees with this message, we really have to 'keep it super simple,' kind of the PG version of the K.I.S.S. rule.

"Because of the potential for complexity when designing these things, often an owner will just throw their hands up and say, 'You know what, let's just figure it out at the end of the year.' That's when the plan really becomes just discretionary. It's kind of based on how you're feeling at the moment, and it's reactive in its essence.

"And this is the second mistake I've witnessed owners make with incentive plans—they're discretionary. If you have a discretionary plan, you're basically getting to the end of the year, calculating a bonus, and then paying it out. But we're missing a real opportunity here. We can flip the script. If we design the plan using a simple formula and then tell everybody the score along the way, we can actually create opportunities to change behavior during the middle of the game because we have such great data."

"If the company's trending off-track, we can do something about it before it's too late so that when you get to the end of the year, *they* have created the incentive pool that you are paying out. They have done this by driving incremental profit above and beyond a trigger, and this profit becomes earned compensation. This type of incentive plan is not reactive, it's not discretionary or subjective, and it's not an entitlement."

Eddie continued. "So, you can see that the education and the business literacy must go hand in hand with the incentive plan.

"A third common mistake is creating a plan that creates a siloed organization. For example, if you create departmental incentive plans, there's a possibility that you may pit departments against each other. They're going to figure out how to get their bonus, whether it hurts another department or not. This creates unhealthy competition inside your organization; people want to win, and if you design the game in a departmental way, they're going to figure out a way to 'win.' For example, they may not share resources with other departments, they may not play nice, or they may stop communicating. They might hoard people or resources; soon, you have a splintered organization," Eddie explained.

6 MISTAKES

1. TOO COMPLEX
2. DISCRETIONARY
3. SILOS
4. UNATTAINABLE
5. DISCONNECTED
6. NO VALUE

"This is also a critical reason to include all employees in your incentive plan and make it a broad-based incentive plan. Why would we want to include all employees?" Eddie asked.

"Team building?" suggested Bob.

"Exactly, Bob," Eddie said. "As we said earlier, we need to have one vision for the entire organization. We are one team, and we need everyone aligned. We need all the arrows pointing in one direction. Everyone can contribute to the company's profit. And everyone has the potential of subtracting from it as well, depending on the decisions they're making day-in and day-out. So, I strongly encourage you to develop a simple plan that includes everyone.

"The other drawback to siloed incentive plans is that you have to administer all those plans," Eddie said. "Back to David Rock's point, often the implementation itself creates fairness issues. This results in stress, envy, isolation or relatedness issues. For example, I've seen people exclude sales teams from the company-wide incentive plan because they figure, 'Well, salespeople already have their commissions.'"

Eddie paused as his audience nodded. "Rather than taking that position, I encourage you to think about sales commissions as what we call '*Me* Comp.' From an Accountability Chart perspective, a sales seat has a certain compensation structure associated with the expectations of that function in the organization. The seat on The Accountability Chart has a handful of roles that the person who owns a seat is expected to get and want. The seat on The Accountability Chart has meetings that it needs to attend, processes that it needs to follow, and measurables that it needs to hit. There's also compensation associated with that seat, and that's where sales commissions apply. It truly is '*Me* Comp.'

"What we're talking about here, though, with the incentive plan, is '*We* Comp;' it's team compensation, a reward and a celebration when the team wins. This type of plan offers incentives in addition to, and above and beyond the *Me* Comp.

"So that's the third mistake, a siloed organization. The fourth mistake is what I call 'unattainable goals.' Now, this generally appears when the employees perceive that the goals are unattainable because they haven't really been taught about business. They don't know about all the money that may be falling through the cracks. In my experience, everyone in the organization can usually see something in their line of sight that can be done better. We need to create a forum for those ideas to be generated and shared, discussed and solved.

"When employees see how much is potentially falling through the cracks, they start to realize, 'Wow, those goals that are on our V/TO are actually attainable! If we tighten up this area over here, and document these processes over there, and do some training over here, we can actually create a lot more profitability in the company and find the money to fund the incentive plan.' That's when the employees start to see the goals as being truly attainable, and that's motivating for people.

"Now, there is somewhat of an art form to creating enough incentive that people remain interested in playing the game, but not too much of a stretch that they want to give up. It's kind of like the middle of the bell curve—there's a little bit of art and a little bit of science.

"The fifth mistake I see is one we've talked about already: it's this idea of the employees feeling disconnected from the incentive plan. As leaders, we need to consistently help employees understand how their daily activities, weekly measurables, quarterly Rocks, and so forth are all tightly connected to the company's financial performance at the end of the quarter or year. You need to share how the one-year plan is tied to what the employees do every day so that they feel tightly connected to driving that plan. This is not just the leadership team's plan—it's the company's plan. Creating alignment takes consistency, patience, and repetition.

"The sixth mistake I've seen is called 'No Value.' This happens when you get to the end of the year and have a little bit of money left over. You pay out bonuses, and maybe everybody gets a couple hundred bucks. It's not very motivating. Employees certainly don't turn it away, in my experience, but we're missing a real opportunity to create meaningful payout dollars that are formulaic and tied to their behavior," Eddie explained.

"Rather than giving everyone a negligible bonus, think of a range between 5 and 15 percent of wages. Imagine this amount being paid out to your team members at the end of the year; that could represent some pretty meaningful dollars!

"Now, you have to walk before you run, so since we're all playing the long game here, depending on where you're starting, you might be at the lower end of that range in year one, but if the company hits a stretch goal in a year, perhaps there might be some meaningful dollars in there around 10–15 percent of wages. That gets pretty interesting for people and pretty valuable.

"Of course, there are spreadsheets involved here where you're modeling different 'what if' scenarios, but, ultimately, if we can end up somewhere in that wage range with the company still hitting its goals, and we're focused on just one number for simplicity and profitability, people will get meaningful incentives.

"But as one of my clients said, 'You can't quit and stay.' Meaning we need *active* participants here. We need people who think and act like owners and see the business through these new eyes we've talked about. In this way, the employees are actively finding the money to fund the plan. They become active participants in the business's success, and they all share in the celebration at the end of the day."

Eddie took a drink of water before continuing. His audience was engaged and tracking well with his presentation. It seemed like these mistakes were hitting a nerve.

"Let's talk a little bit about incentive plan best practices," he started. "The best practice characteristics are essentially the flip side of the coin of the incentive plan mistakes. But let's go through them one by one just to clarify and answer any questions you might have.

"The first characteristic is certainly the opposite of complexity, which is to say, keep it super simple. We want our incentive plan to be simple in design, easy to explain, easy to understand, and easy to trust. Trust is the key element here. We have such an opportunity to build trust by focusing on one number, for example, profit, which is truly the score at the end of the game. That helps us focus on simplicity.

"The second element of well-designed plans is that they are truly self-funded. They need to drive the value of the business. They need to pay for themselves. As we've discussed, if you design an incentive plan that doesn't pay for itself, you're basically creating what?" Eddie asked.

"Another expense," said Jane.

"Exactly, and none of us want more expenses. Your company's plan certainly has to pay for itself. This also touches back on the Positive Tension curve; if we're trying to move everyone from a mindset of entitlement to a mindset of earning, the concept of self-funded is self-evident in that the incremental profit that's created to fund the plan is created from the changed behavior and the mindsets of the employees. They earn their incentive rather than it being provided as a bonus or a gift," he explained.

"A third characteristic of a well-designed incentive plan is that it has to be about shared targets. This helps us avoid silos and sends a strong message that we are all part of one company. We have one vision, we are one team, we have one operating system, we have one voice, we have one shared target, and we recognize that each of us plays a different role in affecting that target. We certainly want to monitor and measure those departmental measurables, but my suggestion is to not create incentive plans around departmental measurables.

"Let's talk about why I say that. First, a plan based on departmental measurables is very complex and time-consuming to administer. Secondly, you might end up paying out a bonus to a department because they achieved some measurable target, but the company could be losing money or not hitting its goals for some other reason. We don't want to send a mixed message by paying out bonuses when the company's not doing well. So shared targets is a super important message."

BEST PRACTICES

1. SIMPLE
2. SELF-FUNDED
3. SHARED TARGETS
4. THRESHOLD
5. SHAPE EMPLOYEE BEHAVIOR
6. MOTIVATING

Eddie continued. "A fourth best practice is what I call Positive Tension. This relates to the trigger or the threshold that has to be reached before the incentive plan kicks in.

"We need to protect the company and pay the company first. What are some obligations the company has before we consider paying out an incentive?"

"Capital investment," said Miguel.

"Yes, we want to invest in the future, in growth. Great, what are some other things the company needs to account for?"

"Taxes!" said Fred.

"Right! We've got to pay taxes. So almost half of that is gone there."

"Anything else come to mind? What about all the risk you've taken?"

"Return on investment," said Eileen.

"R-O-I," said Eddie. "Why do people take risks?"

"To get a return," continued Eileen.

"And where do all returns on investment come from?" asked Eddie.

"From profit," said Eileen.

"Exactly. So we must have profit to provide the return on investment for the people taking all the risk. Any other obligations the company would want to consider in that threshold?" asked Eddie.

"Debt," said Jane.

"Yes," said Eddie. "We'll want to protect the company by preserving some profit to pay down or retire debt. We want the trigger to be realistic, but we also want to stretch everyone. When we talk about your budget as it relates to the trigger, that will be an important conversation. We want to create enough tension to help people recognize that this is not going to be a layup, but it's not going to be a half-court shot either. So, we've got this threshold or trigger protecting the company, and we can take a percentage of the incremental dollars above that number and set it aside in an incentive pool."

"The fifth element of a well-designed incentive plan is that it really does direct and shape employee behavior. We want the incentive plan to direct all the human energy in your company and to encourage all the arrows to point in the same direction. This is about helping everybody align themselves toward common business goals. We want an ownership culture and an ownership mindset. That requires not only a target to shoot for but also all the tools and training and consistency and leadership and management and resources that help shape employee behavior and direct their human energy toward improving the financial performance of the company."

Eddie paused for his audience to allow this point to sink in. Finally, he continued. "The last point about the incentive plan is it needs to be motivating. It needs to be valuable and perceived as valuable. If you get to the end of the year, you have a little bit of money left over, and everybody gets a couple hundred bucks, it's not going to be super motivating. As I mentioned, we've done a lot of research around this, and we know that a payout in the range of 5 to 15 percent of wages gets pretty interesting for people. When coaching our clients, we're trying to help them look at all these different levers and create a plan that pays out in that range. We recognize that it will never be perfect, but an effective plan will help accomplish these six characteristics."

Eddie glanced at the clock. "And finally, before we break, we've got three ground rules we suggest considering. One of them is that we suggest paying out your plan quarterly. Why would we say quarterly?"

"To reward more frequently?" suggested Dexter.

"That's right: line of sight. When we reward a behavior quickly, we immediately reinforce that behavior, and we are more likely to shape the behavior in the direction we want. It also gives you a chance to share the score more frequently and celebrate progress at your State of the Company Meetings.

"But we don't suggest you pay it all out quarterly. If you pay out these large bonuses in the first two quarters and then your company hits a downturn, you're not going to be able to ask your employees for their bonuses back. So, we typically design incentive plans with a holdback so the company is protected; it is just smart business. If someone leaves before the end of the third quarter, they don't get that payment or the year-end payment. That goes back into the pool and gets distributed to everyone else. We will get into more detail after the break as we look at some examples.

"A second ground rule revolves around payouts, the 'who gets what' question. Payouts can happen in a couple of different ways, and there are two main methods we propose for our clients. They're called Percentage of Wages payout and Equal Payout. I will talk about them briefly here, and then we can talk in more detail as we look at examples and consider the positives and negatives of each method.

"The Percentage of Wages method is the most common way to payout with the plans we design. The bottom line with this method is that everyone gets the same percentage of wages. As a simple example, if we surpass the trigger, and a pool of incentive dollars is generated when we do the payout calculation, it may turn out everyone is getting 5 percent of their wage or 10 percent of their wage. That's pretty common.

"The Equal Payout method is also easy to calculate. You just divide the incentive pool by the number of people participating, but it requires some discussion and consideration because it tends to send a different message to your team. Again, we'll talk through some examples in detail after the break.

"The last ground rule is around changing the plan during the year. This is really a credibility thing. Employees need to understand that this may change from year to year. Your agreement with the employees, though, is that you won't change the plan during the year.

"There are two things I've seen happen. Number one, we get through the first two quarters of a year, we are paying out these huge incentives, and we freak out and raise the targets. We lose a lot of credibility, and often for many years. The trust account turns negative, and it can take a long time to get back to a positive balance.

"The flip side can happen, too. We don't quite hit our targets, but we want to be nice, so we hand out the bonus anyway. What's the message we just sent?"

"That goals don't matter," said Eileen.

"Everyone gets a trophy," said Miguel.

"Right. So, our credibility is shot there, too," Eddie replied. "We want to keep the plan fresh, so how do we do that? One of the ways we'll discuss this is through Challenge Rocks. Some teams have a fun Annual Theme for their company and tie the plan into that.

"Overall, I believe you should reevaluate your incentive plan every year when you go through your budgeting process. You'll want to develop a set of simple guidelines, or ground rules, for your plan, and make sure you communicate those to your team when we roll out the plan."

Eddie continued. "After the break, let's get into some examples of incentive plans from other companies, and we can talk through any questions you have and clarify other nuances and exceptions. You guys ready for a break? Let's take about ten minutes and agree to be back here at the top of the hour."

• • •

Eileen was convinced Eddie could help Swan. At the end of the meeting, she waited in the long line to speak with him—his presentation had a positive effect on most of the roundtable attendees, including John, who was initially resistant to Eddie's ideas.

"That was an inspiring presentation," Eileen said as she finally had an opportunity to speak to Eddie. "We're struggling with our bonus plan at Swan, and I was wondering if you might have time to meet with me and my partner to discuss how we could make it more effective."

Eddie said, "Absolutely."

They exchanged cards and agreed to meet the following week at Swan.

CHAPTER 6

PROFIT WORKS AT SWAN

Eddie was early for the meeting at Swan. Eileen met him at the reception area, and they walked together to the conference room. Eddie found his seat across from Eileen, making small talk while they waited for Vic.

"Thank you for inviting me over, Eileen. I always love talking with companies who are running on EOS—it's just a completely different level of conversation."

"Absolutely," Eileen said, "I really enjoyed your talk last week. So many of the points you made about entitlement mentality and year-end bonuses being perceived as a gift really hit home with me. Vic and I had a Same Page Meeting this past Monday, and we're excited to see how you can help us."

"That's great," said Eddie. "I'll tell you what, entitlement mentality touches a nerve for so many entrepreneurs. It's one of those mindsets that I feel like we created but that we also have the power to minimize. It's a real opportunity for us as individuals and for companies."

Vic hustled through the doorway and closed the door behind him. "Sorry I'm a little late," said Vic. "Not my M.O. of course, as we've really gotten good at starting and ending our meetings on time. Speaking of which, how long do you see us meeting today?"

"Hi, Vic," Eddie said, shaking Vic's extended hand. "Very nice to meet you. Eddie Stevens from ProfitWorks. We've allocated an hour for our meeting. Does that still work for you?"

"Yes, that's great," said Vic.

"Great." They settled into their seats around the table.

Eddie started, "Well, if you're ready, and since we all speak EOS, let's jump in and agree on a quick agenda for our Discover Meeting. In our short time together, I'd love for us to share enough information with each other to discover whether or not I can help you.

"I'll start by sharing a little information about ProfitWorks and about me, and then we can talk about Swan Services, especially as it relates to incentive plans and developing what we call an Ownership Culture. After that, I'll share the ProfitWorks Solution and our proven process to help you design and launch a self-funded incentive plan. If that sounds alright, how about I start by telling you a little about my background?"

Vic and Eileen nodded.

"Great," said Eddie. "I started ProfitWorks back in 1996 with my brother. Our father was on quite a few advisory boards in our town and spent a lot of time with entrepreneurs. An entrepreneur himself, he saw a pattern in what these business owners were saying when it came to their employees' understanding of profit. He thought perhaps there might be a business opportunity to teach employees about business, finance, and basic economics. My brother and I decided to start the business after doing a little bit of research, and we developed a training and consulting business that helped companies enroll their employees in the financial picture and help them begin to think and act like owners.

"Over a few years, we were exposed to quite a few different methods of gainsharing and profit sharing, different formulas, and other incentive plan designs, and we realized that the business education we were providing helped sort of wake up the employees to seeing the business with new eyes.

"As the employees were given tools like Scorecards and measurables, and in some cases, gamifying improvements of the measurables, our clients inevitably found increased profitability. This is key: the employees created increased profitability, and the owners felt comfortable sharing some of that incremental profit in an incentive plan because it had essentially paid for itself.

"Our business took a lot of twists and turns over the years, and we've ultimately settled on a very simple model that helps entrepreneurial organizations implement this solution.

"In 2012, I was introduced to the Entrepreneurial Operating System, EOS, by one of my clients, and I decided to pursue that full-time. During the pandemic, I took time to write a book about all my experiences. It led to a resurgence of interest for entrepreneurs who wanted to create an ownership culture and really tap into the unrealized potential of their employees.

"Since 1996, we've worked with hundreds of companies and thousands of employees to design self-funded incentive plans and teach business literacy workshops. When working with clients, we help them with three things we call Simple, Self-funded, and Supported: the 3 S's.

"*Simple* means keeping the incentive plan simple in design. When the plans are simple, they are easy to launch and understand, which means your employees will trust the plan. Simple also means implementing our business literacy training, which simplifies the complex topic of financial education for employees. Also, Simple aligns beautifully with EOS's basic philosophy."

Vic continued nodding at Eddie's explanation while Eileen took notes.

"*Self-funded* means the incentive plan pays for itself. When the workforce is business-literate, they have a new perspective on how precious profit is. Employees become active participants in finding the money to fund the plan. They use Tension Tools like Scorecards, measurables, Challenge Rocks, and more, so they are actually creating and earning the pool of dollars in the incentive plan.

"*Supported* means we coach and provide training for you for as long as you need us and for as long as we're adding value to help your leaders, your internal champions, on an ongoing basis. We arm them with the confidence, content, and all the tools they'll need to teach and reinforce the plan as part of their leadership role on a continuous basis.

"Ultimately, we get to the point where you realize the untapped potential in your workforce. Everyone in your company is thinking and acting like an owner towards creating wealth, not only for themselves but also for the company. It's an arduous journey, but it's certainly worth the effort!

"We mostly work with entrepreneurial organizations with between 10 and 250 employees. They are running on an operating system, ideally EOS. Our best clients are open to some level of transparency and are interested in and willing to share more information with their employees. They also want to share profits with their employees, celebrate winning as a team, and help them feel that pride of accomplishment. They believe there is untapped potential in their workforce, and they care for, respect, and are willing to invest in their employees.

"That's why I'm excited to be here today with you, sharing the ProfitWorks model and helping you build a culture of ownership thinkers," Eddie said.

"That's my professional story. Personally, my wife and I have been married for over 25 years, and we have three awesome kids. We are empty nesters now, which is a new state of happiness for us. Don't get me wrong, we loved raising the kids, but this new chapter is certainly a fun one for us as well," he concluded.

Vic said, "Cool, Eddie. Eileen shared quite a bit of what you shared in the roundtable last week. In the interest of time, can you jump ahead to how we might work together?"

"Absolutely, Vic, and thank you. As I'm going through the model, I'd like to learn a little bit about you and Swan Services as well, so I will ask you some questions along the way," Eddie said.

"Great," said Vic.

"First, tell me a little bit of the history of Swan Services. How old is the company? How many employees? How many are on the leadership team? What's the revenue goal for this year, that kind of thing," Eddie asked.

"Eileen, you wanna take this one?" Vic asked.

"Sure," said Eileen.

Eileen proceeded to give the background of how Swan Services was founded, how she and Vic shared the passion for their technology consulting work, and how they loved the impact they were having in the market and with their clients.

She also shared how they had hit a ceiling a few years ago and decided to implement EOS when a friend of hers, Miguel, whom Eddie had met at the meeting, had introduced her to Alan, their EOS Implementer. He helped them get up and running on EOS.

Since implementing EOS, Swan's revenues had climbed over 30 percent, and their profits had steadily increased as well. "Next year," said Eileen, "we're targeting $10 million in sales at a 12 percent profit. We've never hit 12 percent, but honestly, we feel like we should be closer to 15 percent profit if we really start to address some of the deeper issues at the company, the growing pains."

Eileen shared that they had 35 employees and that six of them were on the leadership team. She and Vic, the owners, were included.

"That's great," said Eddie. "Really helpful. Historically, as you've been doing State of the Company Meetings with your workforce, what does that typically look like?"

"Well," said Eileen, "we typically do those quarterly, and we've been pretty consistent about it. We followed Alan's advice with the agenda, which is generally 'past, present, and future,' so we're telling them about the last 90 days, and we're telling them kind of year-to-date details: updates, new hires, new accounts, and so forth. Then we share the V/TO with them."

"And with that V/TO," said Eddie, "how much of that do you share?"

"That's actually what prompted this meeting," said Vic. "We kind of zip through that, assuming everybody's getting it. After the Q&A at the last meeting, we realized there was a weak link. I think it's starting to affect morale and could lead to turnover or other culture issues."

"That's not uncommon," said Eddie. "It's easy for us to assume that if somebody's on a leadership team or if they're well-educated, they must automatically understand finance. But it's not always the case, certainly."

"I guess that's why we're talking," said Eileen, smiling.

"That's right," said Eddie. "So, how much financial information do you share with the team?"

"Well, on the V/TO, we share sales, basically. We share the number of whales or big projects, over $100K," Vic answered.

"Have you ever shared gross margin or net profit?" Eddie asked.

"It was on there when we first started sharing the V/TO, but we took it off after a few meetings because we felt like people really didn't understand it," said Vic.

"Tell me more about that," prompted Eddie.

Eileen jumped in. "To tell you the truth, Eddie, we never really explained profit to them. I guess we didn't want to get off-topic in the meeting. We felt like it would take longer to teach them about it than it would to just remove the information from the V/TO."

"But you still track that information in your quarterlies and annuals with the leadership team?" asked Eddie.

They nodded.

"So, essentially, you have two V/TOs: one for the leadership team and one for everyone else because you redact some information from the leadership team V/TO?"

"I guess that's right," said Vic, "but I never really thought about it like that."

"That's okay," said Eddie, "but if we're going to build an incentive plan around a critical measurable like profit, it's going to make sense for everyone to understand what profit is, how it works, why it's important, why they should care, and so forth. Do you agree?"

"Oh, absolutely," said Eileen. "We would love to share more financial information with our employees, but we need help to understand the best way to do that."

"Sure," said Eddie. "That's where I come in. A few more questions, if that's okay." They both nodded.

"Can you tell me a little bit about your experience with incentive plans, bonus plans, gainsharing, and so forth?" asked Eddie.

Vic said, "Let me try this one, Eileen, okay?"

"Sure," said Eileen.

"We've always tried to do something at the end of the year," said Vic. "You know, to kind of share some of the upside when we've had a good year. And everybody really appreciates that . . . or seems to. A few people say thank you, I must admit.

"We try to do it around the holidays because we know people appreciate having a little extra money when they're celebrating with their families, spending a lot of money on gifts, travel, food, and so forth."

"That's very common," said Eddie.

"The problem I see," said Eileen, "is that the bonuses we've been giving out are very disconnected from everybody's job. I think our annual bonus plan is perceived more as a gift for our team at the end of the year."

"So they don't feel like they've earned it?" said Eddie.

"That's right, and they get it every year," said Vic, "regardless of how we do. Eileen and I try to find a way to scrounge up some extra cash, and one year, we even borrowed money on our line of credit so that we could pay out the end-of-year bonus," Vic admitted.

"How did that make you feel?" asked Eddie, knowingly.

"We hadn't really reflected on it," said Vic, "because it's just something we've always done."

"And that's where I think entitlement mentality has crept into our culture," added Eileen.

"Entitlement mentality," said Vic. "Ugh. That's such an annoyance. If we have developed a group of entitled employees . . . ," he trailed off. "They're such great people," he said, "and I know they don't mean to feel entitled, but maybe we've created that kind of environment here through just paying out bonuses every year regardless of our performance."

"It's easy for people to slip into entitlement mentality because often owners and leaders aren't explaining the

Why. It really takes intention and time to formulate an incentive plan that truly changes people's behavior," Eddie said comfortingly. "It requires us to commit to a culture where we are more transparent about the performance of the company and our financials: the score, if you will. We also have to commit to sharing both good and bad news," he added.

"Vic," said Eileen, "the other thing you mentioned to me a few weeks ago was that if we start sharing more financial information with the team, they're going to want more money, and this topic came up at the roundtable from John, who is completely opposed to sharing information with his employees."

"Yeah, that's right," said Vic. "How do we handle that?"

"There's irony to that," said Eddie, "because once they realize profit is more like 10 or 12 percent, they're not thinking 'I want more money,' they're thinking, 'Wow, that's a lot less than I thought!' and, ideally, if we do it in the right way, they are motivated to help figure out how to increase it.

"When you tie an incentive plan to the bottom line," Eddie continued, "with education as required context, they become more tuned into that number and try to figure out how to add to it so they can put more money in their own pockets. The key, I've found," said Eddie, "is that you can't just share the information once and expect everyone to retain it. Just like we say in EOS, people have to hear something seven times for them to hear it for the first time. It's the same thing with business literacy. *You* might look at income statements and cash flow statements every month . . ."

"And I'm still trying to understand those!" laughed Vic.

"That's right!" said Eddie. "And they might look at it once a quarter on a screen and just have to be reminded about how the math works. I think sometimes on leadership teams, we assume that everybody already understands this stuff, so we gloss over it without stopping to define how we got to profit.

"The way I see it," said Eddie, "is that not sharing the information with a team we respect is just a missed opportunity. We know these people are smart—we hired them! If we've done the hard work of holding people accountable to our clearly stated expectations around core values, their roles, and making sure they really have everything they need to be star performers, it's fair to believe they can understand this type of information. What we're saying is that we really love our people, and we just want to establish a simple incentive formula that's easy to explain and easy to understand."

"So, we need to give everyone in the company, all 35 people, the tools, training, and resources to become active participants in looking for and finding the money that will help fund their incentive plan. In this way, the Swan team becomes a team that thinks and acts like owners. Over time, what happens is that the employees start to take better care of the business, look for improvements in operational efficiencies, make suggestions, take Rocks, document processes, hold each other accountable, and fund their incentive plan.

"Ideally, they're taking home more money so they can take better care of themselves as well. It really becomes a lot of fun as the culture shifts to an ownership culture. It's lighter, and there's more laughter, but we're all also focused, productive, and driven," Eddie explained. "It truly becomes a philosophy where we take better care of *We*, the V/TO represents our 'one company vision,' EOS becomes our language and our one operating system, and we have *one* incentive plan from which we all benefit."

"It really is about trying to get all the arrows pointing in the same direction," said Eileen.

Eddie nodded. "Alright, that gives me everything I need. I do want to ask you one last question: Is there anything I should have asked about, or is there anything that you would like to backfill that I didn't cover?"

Vic and Eileen looked at each other.

Eileen said, smiling, "How fast can we get something designed and launched, Eddie, from your experience?"

"Yeah, the natives are restless," said Vic.

"We have some options," said Eddie. "If you're OK with me answering that question more specifically when I get to the process step, that would be great."

"Great," said Eileen.

"There is one other thing," said Vic. "Eileen and I started this company together a long time ago because we really believe in people. We see so much potential in this team, so much untapped potential and unrealized opportunity. We really want to create a great company. We know it's a really good company right now, but as achievers, we know that with the right team, we can do so much more. We're already having a huge impact on so many lives both inside and outside the company, and I think we can keep up that trend if we do this just right. Neither Eileen nor I are very impressed with some of the entitlement mentality we've heard displayed over the last several years, so I'm excited to see where we can take this. I feel like if we can help everyone at Swan develop an earning mindset, it will not only help the company but also help them as individuals. They will be able to take better care of themselves and their families."

Eddie and Eileen let Vic's comments sink in.

"With that, I'd like to go to step three now and get into the ProfitWorks Solution with you," Eddie announced.

Eddie handed Eileen and Vic each a copy of a one-page document called the ProfitWorks Solution.

"What you've got in front of you now is what we call the ProfitWorks Solution, which has three elements to it. Starting in the upper right, the first component is called the Operating System. This is EOS, which you are already masters of." Eddie smiled.

"I wouldn't say 'masters,'" said Eileen.

"Hey, Alan set you guys up for success! You made a great decision hiring an Implementer rather than trying to do it on your own," Eddie said. "The self-implementing companies I have met with when we're talking about ProfitWorks often miss much of the nuance to EOS. They're not sure if they're doing it right. They aren't as disciplined with their use of the tools, either. It's not that it doesn't work; it's just that it usually takes a lot longer to get the results.

"It sounds like you're seeing positive changes happening at Swan that are strengthening the alignment around the Vision in your organization and helping you gain traction, meaning you're increasing the discipline and accountability, and you've created a healthy, functional, cohesive leadership team."

Eddie continued. "One of the big lessons we learned early on was that implementing an incentive plan and the business literacy tools without a firm foundation of alignment, discipline and accountability, especially at the leadership team level, is a recipe for failure. Essentially, you'd be designing and rolling out an incentive plan for an organization that is not in alignment. It's not an incentive plan problem when the incentive plan doesn't work; that's actually a leadership problem."

"The second element is called the No Entitlement Incentive Plan. There are three disciplines, or tools, to strengthen that component. They are: Simple, Self-Funded, and Supported."

"At this stage of implementation, we act as your incentive plan coaches. After we gather a little bit of information from you, we put together the first draft of your plan, which we will review together. We'll shoot holes in it together and modify it to get it to the point where you're confident and ready to launch it," Eddie explained.

"This is where Simplicity comes into play in a big way. Our role as incentive plan coaches is to help you keep Simplicity in mind when designing the plan: 'Are we able to communicate the plan easily?' 'Is everyone who's involved in the plan able to understand it?' We want the employees to trust it, and if the plan is too complex, they won't trust it, and it's much more of an uphill battle to gain traction.

"The reason we called our plan the No Entitlement Incentive Plan is because the ideal result is that the incentive plan motivates your employees and directs their energy into improving the financial performance of the company. If we design and roll out an incentive plan, but employee behavior hasn't changed, all we've created is entitlement and another expense. We don't want that, of course. So that's where our years of expertise come in; we coach you through it.

"The third element of the ProfitWorks Solution is called the Missing Link. Once you've got the plan designed and we've co-created this simple, self-funded incentive plan, the Missing Link becomes the key to it being successful. There are three disciplines to strengthen the Missing Link. They are Profit Education, Tension Tools, and 7 Times.

"Profit Education is critical to the success of the incentive plan and is something that our best clients start and end up doing forever. It becomes part of their culture. We have a couple of tools to help you do the Profit Education piece effectively, including an online Masterclass to which our clients have unlimited access. The Masterclass is a library of videos and downloadable 'train the trainer' materials that allow you and your leaders, or any Champions inside your organization, to familiarize themselves with teaching core business fundamentals. The materials also provide tools for driving improvement in the organization to fund the incentive plan. Your leaders and managers will become the critical champions for providing the missing link to the rest of your organization.

"The second discipline under the Missing Link is called Tension Tools. If you remember the bell curve from our meeting, Eileen, which is the basis for the entire ProfitWorks philosophy, you'll recall that at the middle of the bell curve lives some level of tension, the stretch, that leads to higher levels of performance in the organization.

"Some of the Tension Tools you already have in place through EOS. These are tools like Rocks, Scorecards, measurables, Level 10 Meetings, to-do lists, Issues Lists, a 10-Year Target™, and more.

"We also have added Challenge Rocks and even the trigger, established in the incentive plan, as additional important Tension Tools. Using Tension Tools on a continual basis becomes a reinforcement mechanism to provide a missing link for your No-Entitlement Incentive Plan.

"The last discipline under the Missing Link is called 7 Times or 7x. This is a reference to the idea that people have to hear something seven times for them to hear it for the first time. It's sort of a tongue-in-cheek way of saying 'repeat forever.' We will coach you, on a consistent basis, to have regular, formal communication methods with your workforce to not only reinforce how their daily efforts, activities, and decisions can affect the incentive plan but also to communicate the score.

"We'll ask, 'How are we doing this year against the plan?' We want to make sure people understand that when an incentive plan payout occurs at the end of the time period, it's through their efforts and their activities and their changed behavior that incremental profit has been driven to the incentive pool; it's not a gift from Vic and Eileen."

Eddie continued. "So that's the model and the tools. Any questions about any of that?"

"What's the bell curve you're talking about?" asked Vic.

Eddie explained the Positive Tension curve he shared at the roundtable so Vic could understand the philosophy and psychology behind ProfitWorks. Then he said, "With that, I'd like to move to the implementation process. Like you said, Eileen, how do we get started on this? And how long does it take? If you flip over the card, we can walk through the proven process: the exact way we do what we do," he explained.

PROFITWORKS PROCESS

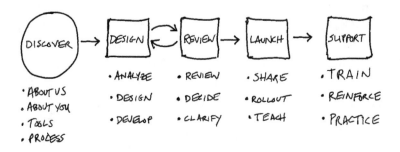

"The first step in the process is the Discover meeting, which is what we're doing here today. After this, if it would be helpful, I can get you a proposal that outlines the steps and the fee arrangements."

"That would be great," said Eileen.

"Provided we move forward, the next step in the process is called Design. In the Design step, after we've gathered a little bit of information from you, analyzed your Financial Trends, and designed a first draft of your incentive plan, we will schedule a time to review the initial design together. That can happen pretty quickly, actually, depending on when we get your financial information.

"That next step in the process is called Review. This is essentially an hour-long meeting during which we will review the first draft of the incentive plan together. We'll decide on various plan design options like the profit trigger, how we are paying out the plan, how often we are paying out the plan, and the pluses and minuses of all these options.

"At this step of the process, we'll also clarify timing and other options for communicating the incentive plan. Additionally, as part of this Review step, we will develop content you can use when you launch the incentive plan to the Swan team. This includes slides and an incentive plan design document. Some teams ask their employees to sign a document to indicate their commitment to the process.

"The fourth step in the ProfitWorks Process is called Launch. In this step, to give important context to the incentive plan, we'll want to teach some profit education and some basic business literacy, as it allows employees to begin to understand the concept of how the profit trigger was established. It gets them talking about ideas for driving improved profitability.

"During the Launch, you will roll out the incentive plan, keeping it as simple as possible. You'll begin to set the stage for the fact that you'll be reinforcing the incentive plan on a continual basis with the Tension Tools and meeting disciplines you already have, namely your State of the Company and departmental Level 10 Meetings."

Eddie continued. "The last step of the process is called Support. As part of our relationship, you'll have access to our online ProfitLink Masterclass™. Lastly, we will periodically be checking in on your progress, holding you accountable for supporting the plan, and be available as a resource to address any challenges you may be having with the program.

"The process is guaranteed," Eddie explained, "meaning that at the end of the first year, if your ProfitWorks engagement is not self-funded, we will provide free quarterly coaching for the next year.

"If you'd like to get started, like I said, I will send you the financial intake form." Eddie paused. "We would welcome the opportunity to be your guide for this journey we're going to take together. We're available for any questions you may have along the way. And it's that simple to get moving. Any questions?"

Vic and Eileen looked at each other.

"I don't think we can put this off," said Vic. "After Todd's question and the Q&A after the last state of the company, we need to do something."

Eileen said, "Eddie, with you guiding us on this, I think it will give us more confidence and more credibility than us doing it alone."

"It's similar to us hiring Alan to help us get up and running on EOS," said Vic.

"Great, I'll get the ball rolling!" said Eddie. "You're going to be so glad we're partnering up."

CHAPTER 7

A SIMPLE PLAN

Eileen received an email from Eddie that included a simple agreement and a blank financial intake form requesting five years of historical financial information. She forwarded the email to Jeff in finance and asked him to fill it out and return it to Eddie within 24 hours. She wanted to keep the project on track so they could launch next year's incentive plan before the end of the year. She figured that if she could always keep the ball in Eddie's court, she could keep the project moving faster.

She signed and returned Eddie's agreement and let him know that Jeff would be getting him the financial information shortly. She also asked Eddie to propose a few dates when they could review the first draft of their incentive plan.

When Eddie received the information from Jeff, he spent time creating the first draft of Swan's new incentive plan, testing different triggers, and experimenting with different payout methods based on what Vic and Eileen had shared so he could share several ideas with Vic and Eileen in their upcoming meeting.

He also prepared a financial trend analysis of charts that illustrated Swan Services' financial performance, using several different measurables.

Eddie knew that when employees are first learning about a company's financial performance, it's a lot less threatening to see the information in a chart than it is to see it in a spreadsheet with lots of numbers. The other great thing about sharing charts with employees is that they can clearly see trends in the financials that help start conversations about what was going on in those time periods that created different outcomes, such as a sharp increase in sales or a sharp decrease in gross margin, along with other types of outlier results from the past.

Last, Eddie started compiling slides that Vic and Eileen would use when they launched the plan.

Within a week of their first meeting, Eileen and Vic jumped on a call with Eddie to talk through the initial draft. Eileen was hopeful and excited about what to expect.

Eddie started. "Thanks for joining me today. I've got some ideas for you and some questions as well, and I'm going to edit things in real-time to show you the consequences of various design decisions you make. Real-time edits allow you to consider your choices more quickly and make faster decisions. I will also be sharing the pluses and minuses of your decisions from my experience as well. Just a reminder: There is no such thing as perfect. We're trying to keep it simple, to protect the company first, and to create enough of an incentive that people connect the dots between what they do every day and the potential incentive payouts."

With that, Eddie screen-shared the first draft of the plan.

"Eileen, Jeff shared that the budget calls for 12 percent profit on sales of $10 million next year. Is that still accurate?" Eddie asked.

"That's right," said Eileen.

"Great, and you also mentioned that you and Vic feel like 15 percent profit should be attainable if we were hitting on all cylinders?"

"At least!" said Vic. "Truly, in a few years, as the mix of business evolves, and our team really starts following all the processes that we've spent so much time documenting, I could see us closing in on a 20 percent bottom line."

"That's great," said Eddie. "What I've got modeled here for next year is a profit trigger that reflects a 10 percent bottom line. That's before taxes, before next year's reinvestment you mentioned, and before the return on investment that you two shared with me that you want to take home next year for taking all the risk. Seeing as you don't have any debt, which is great, that's not an issue right now."

"If our budget is 12 percent," asked Vic, "why would you start the trigger at anything less than that?"

"That's a great question," said Eddie. "The psychology behind this is that if you hit the budget, there's something for everyone to share in, but it's not necessarily life-changing dollars. So, meeting the budget is hitting expectations, and for hitting expectations, there's a small but somewhat meaningful payout."

"Now, if you exceed the budget, and you can see that I've set a stretch goal here of 15 percent of sales, you can see what that does to the payout. Everyone would essentially be getting 7 percent of their wages if you guys hit 15 percent profit. If you don't hit 10 percent, which is what you hit last year, there is no payout in this model. This is where the trigger creates positive tension for your company, and this also illustrates the self-funding nature of the plan."

Eileen asked, "Would it make sense to cap this plan? Like, what if we hit 25 percent profit or something?"

"We can certainly cap the plan," answered Eddie. "Psychologically, we want to create enough of a payout amount that it gets everyone's attention but not so much that we're leaving money on the table, if you will. There's a point of diminishing returns where you're actually

overpaying on incentive, but you're not getting the com-
mensurate increase in performance with each additional
dollar of incentive payout. It's a bit of an art finding that
point, but, again, if we're paying out between 5 and 15
percent of wages for surpassing our goals, that generally
gets everybody pretty jazzed," Eddie explained.

"Another reason owners often cap an incentive plan is
if they foresee some upcoming investment requirements
and they don't want to cripple the company from future
investments to grow.

"Many times, employee-owned companies also cap the
incentive plan because the long game they're playing as an
employee-owned company is the retirement plan that the
ESOP provides. In this situation, the annual incentive plan
offers a short-term line of sight, while the ESOP provides
that long-term line of sight. Based on those ideas, what
are your thoughts about capping the plan?" asked Eddie.

Vic said, "In year one, I like the idea of capping the
plan at like 20 percent of wages or something. What do
you think, Eileen?"

Eileen said, "Yeah, I agree. If sales continue to hockey
stick like Sue is predicting, we're going to need to hire
some folks, in operations especially."

"Great," said Eddie. "That's helpful. Let me illustrate
what that looks like here." Eddie changed a few numbers on
the spreadsheet, and Vic and Eileen could see the changes.

"You can see that above the trigger, we're sharing 30
percent of incremental profits in the incentive pool. I
chose that number to show you what it does to the wages
that would be paid out. There's no magic to that—I'm
just trying to get the payout amount into a range that is
meaningful and valuable for an employee."

Eddie changed the percent share to 40 percent above
the trigger, and Vic and Eileen could see the incentive

pool change to 7 percent of wages if they hit their stretch goal. "I can also show you what it would look like if we increase the trigger to 12 percent profit."

"No, I like your point about getting something for hitting budget," said Vic. "That way, we can stay in alignment with past years but still have our payout philosophy based on a formula, so it's not subjective."

"Ok," said Eddie, "I'll keep the profit trigger at 10 percent."

"This assumes that we have fairly logical wages for each position at the company, right?" asked Eileen.

"It does," said Eddie. "Remember, what we're talking about here is the We Comp stuff. Would you say you have a fairly organized Me Comp structure?"

"We do, generally," said Eileen. "There may be a few folks whose wages need to be adjusted slightly, but we can handle that offline."

"Good," said Eddie. He took a breath before he continued. "Let's talk through a few ideas for payout method and frequency. For the payout method, last week, we talked about two ideas: a percentage of wages formula or an equal payout method. Have you talked through your preferences on that?"

"We have," said Eileen. "Since we have such a small group and a fairly flat organization right now, we wanted to ask you your opinion. What if we do an equal payout next year and see how that goes? If it's effective, maybe we keep it. If not, we can change to a percentage of wages. Can you advise us on that?"

"Absolutely," said Eddie. "The most common method I've seen is a percentage of wages: everyone getting the same percent of their wage. It's pretty easy to calculate and pretty easy to teach everyone. Most people agree that a wage is tied to a seat and the relative value the seat brings to the company. The fact is if someone is not happy with their base wage, they need to add more value: acquire new skills, increase their capacity, and so forth. So, an incentive that follows this logic is pretty common."

Eddie went on. "Like you said, when you have a smaller, flatter organization, it can be impactful to divide the incentive pool by the number of people and pay it out so that everyone gets the same dollar amount. There are some interesting effects to this, as you can imagine. Number one, everyone knows what everyone else is getting, so it creates a message of transparency, unity, and camaraderie: we're all in this together. Also, when an employee is getting the same dollar amount as a manager, it sends a message that everyone is important. Now, managers might feel like it's unfair. But oftentimes, they see the bigger picture and the positive impact on morale, and they get behind it. It's certainly very easy to calculate and administer, and it's very easy to communicate.

"From a peer-to-peer accountability standpoint, you'll likely ask questions such as, 'Do we need to hire an extra person?' or, 'Can we balance the workload differently?' Our denominator needs to stay relatively small, so these are great conversations to have. I've observed that there tends to be less tolerance for wrong person/wrong seat issues when everyone is kind of drinking from the same well; they really want an equal level of accountability," Eddie said.

"That's interesting," replied Vic. "It seems a little like socialism," he laughed, "like everyone is equal."

"Yeah, it's not for everyone," said Eddie, "but the peer-to-peer accountability and the discipline that you, Eileen, and your leadership team show by not subsidizing poor performance sends a very strong message."

"Talk to us a little bit about the percentage of wages payout method," said Eileen.

"That's the one I've got modeled here," said Eddie. "Basically, we know that total wages are around $2.8 million, and we know what percent of those total wages each person's wage is through simple math. Essentially, that product is multiplied by the incentive pool and the result is that each person gets the same percentage of wages."

"Is it possible to blend the two?" asked Eileen. "Like 60 percent of the pool is paid out based on a percentage of wages, and 40 percent of the pool is paid out equally?"

"Absolutely," said Eddie. "I've got that modeled over on this sheet." He clicked to a different tab.

"The caution is that it's a little bit more complex to explain. The benefit is that you keep people's focus on both their individual contributions as well as the team's performance as a unit, and you can walk a line that balances both."

"Oh, I like that," said Eileen. "Vic, what do you think about a blended payout approach?"

"I hear Eddie on his point about creeping toward complexity, but I like the balance of the We with the Me," he answered.

"Great," said Eddie. "Why don't we keep going down this line of thinking and talk about how frequently the payout should occur? Have you had a chance to discuss whether you want to stay with an annual payout or move to a more frequent quarterly payout?"

Eileen answered, "Vic and I discussed that at our Same Page Meeting on Monday, and we like the idea of this year, trying a quarterly payout with a holdback, as you recommended at our business roundtable."

"Great," said Eddie, "let me get to that tab in the spreadsheet, and I can illustrate for you what that might look like based on the assumptions we've modeled with the trigger and the percent share above the trigger. Also, keep in mind that the sheets that we're looking at now really aren't what we share when we're rolling the plan out. This is the backstage back of the napkin modeling that we're doing to help us through the thinking and decision process for the incentive plan.

"Vic, since you weren't at the roundtable, let me give you some context here. The idea is that at the end of each quarter, provided we've surpassed that quarter's trigger, we calculate the incentive pool and pay out half of it. We do that in the first three quarters of the year, and then we true it up at the end of the year. The other half of the first three quarters' payout is 'banked' to the end of the year to protect the company in the event of a downturn later in the year," Eddie explained.

"Even though the payout amounts can be smaller in the first three quarters of the year, there's somewhat of a retention method built into the psychology of this payout method, and, because it's rear-end loaded, it also stays aligned with that end-of-year bump that you are historically used to paying out."

"I think we like that," said Vic.

"Okay," said Eddie, "we've got about ten minutes left on the call, and if you're good with it, I'd like to spend some time talking a little bit about the launch process."

Eddie led the discussion, helping Eileen and Vic agree on a date for the launch—two weeks out—and a location for the event, which they agreed would be at the Walker Art Center. They asked Eddie to be present for a bit of it so he could provide context of the ProfitWorks philosophy to the team.

As they adjourned, Eddie scheduled one last meeting the following week to walk through the final version of the incentive plan, the Launch Event Objectives and Agenda, as well as the Launch slides and exercises.

CHAPTER 8

CONNECTING THE DOTS

Eddie, Vic, and Eileen met at the Walker Art Center an hour prior to the launch event. While Eileen set up the laptop and tested the slides and the technology, Eddie and Vic made sure the tables, chairs, handouts, whiteboard, and flipchart were all set. There were six round tables set for five to six people per table. Eddie had asked for this setup so they could do a small group activity during the launch.

As the Swan employees started to trickle in, Eddie could hear an exciting buzz around this end-of-the-year meeting, hearing about the plan and bonuses for the next year. Eileen had planned a buffet after the meeting, as well as a few cocktails with the team so they could hang out and decompress.

As soon as everyone was settled, Eileen, at the front of the room, kicked it off. "This is a really exciting time for us at Swan Services. We're excited to welcome you here to our End of the Year Launch Party. If you've been here for a few years, you know that we typically have a party at the end of the year to recap and get pumped up for the next year. This year, we've invited a guest to join us. His name is Eddie Stevens, and his company is called ProfitWorks."

Eileen paused for the applause as Eddie stood for acknowledgment before she continued. "I met Eddie a few weeks ago at one of my business roundtable events. He was talking to the group on the topic of incentive plans. As you may remember from our recent State of the Company Meeting, the subject of end of year bonuses came up. To be honest, this is something Vic and I have struggled with for years. As you may know, the payouts we've made in the past have been discretionary, and quite honestly, Vic and I used to look at them as sort of an end-of-the-year gift for everyone for all your hard work. That's certainly not going to change, but we want to tie the payouts—and Eddie would correct me on this, it's really the payout potential or the payout opportunity—we want to tie that to all the work we've done through the year. In the past, when we got to the end of the year and hit our one-year goals, we failed to truly tie the bonuses to that performance. What happens is that it becomes somewhat of an entitlement or an expectation."

Eileen continued. "That's our fault, but we want to correct that today when we talk about next year's incentive plan. The good news is you'll each be seeing bonuses in your next paycheck. The other piece of good news is that—provided we hit our goals next year—this trend will continue. We also want to help you see that if our performance exceeds our expectations, that payout can be a lot richer for all of us. So, I'm going to turn it over to Eddie to provide some context and background for you. Then we'll teach a little bit about the income statement, or the P&L, and we'll do a group activity as we share the incentive plan for next year. Please help me welcome Eddie Stevens—let's give him a warm Swan Services welcome."

The group gave an energetic round of applause as Eddie approached the front of the room.

Eddie said, "Thank you, Eileen, and thank you, Vic. I really appreciate being here with you all today. This is a subject that's near and dear to my heart, and I hope it's meaningful for you as well.

"I won't belabor my background too much, but suffice it to say I'm an EOS Implementer, and I know you all know what EOS is, and you're big fans. My history prior to EOS is on the subject that we're going to talk about today, which is creating an organization of employees who think and act like owners and who also share in profit improvement through a self-funded incentive plan.

"What I'd like to start with is something we call the blank income statement exercise. We've got you guys set up in groups at your tables. In the middle of each table are handouts for each of you. So, grab one of those, and let's get this started."

A low murmur and a shuffling of papers broke the silence while Eileen and Vic watched with hopeful anticipation.

"Before you do any writing on this," Eddie said, " let me just define some of the terms on here and help you walk through this. Then, we'll give you a few minutes as a group to work on a final product for your table. You can write on these, make them your own, and have some fun while we learn a little bit about this.

"Let's start by defining an income statement. Anybody know what an income statement is and why we need it?" Eddie asked.

In such a large group, Eddie knew that it might be tough to pull answers out of the team at the beginning of the event, but he also knew that if he, Vic, and Eileen did their jobs right, everybody would be laughing and learning by the end.

"If it's the same thing as a P&L, my guess is an income statement shows profit and loss," said Todd.

"That's fantastic," said Eddie, "and you're right on track for our definition because, in order to get to the idea of profit, we first have to sell something, right?

"At Swan Services, you guys sell technology consulting projects; that's simply called sales," Eddie wrote the word Sales on a whiteboard that was brought in for the event. "Is sales the same thing as profit?" he asked.

"No, you have to subtract costs," said Kristina.

"Excellent," said Eddie. "Tell me more about that. What's your name?"

"Kristina," she replied.

Eddie nodded.

"Costs in our company are basically people costs," said Kristina. "It's all of us."

"That's great, Kristina," said Eddie. Beneath Sales on the whiteboard, he wrote "Expenses" with a minus sign in front of it. Then, he drew a line under it. "When we subtract all of our expenses from our sales, what do you call what's leftover?"

"Profit," said several people in unison.

$$
\begin{aligned}
\text{SALES} \\
- \text{EXPENSES} \\
\hline
\text{PROFIT}
\end{aligned}
$$

"Excellent," said Eddie. "So, an income statement, which is also called a P&L, shows the amount of sales, costs, and profit of a business over a given period of time.

What that means is that an income statement can be generated for a month, a quarter, or a year. It's representative of some period of time.

"With your blank income statement in front of you, I'd like you to have a conversation with your group. Identify a scribe who will write down your final answers on a sheet that will be turned in."

Eddie gave the group a few minutes to designate a scribe.

"Scribes, at the top of your sheet, go ahead and write down a group name—any name you wish—but keep it clean!" Eddie said as several folks laughed. "I'll let you get started in a second, but I want to define the terms on this sheet. Once you start, you'll take a stab at filling this in for this past year. What would you guess those numbers are, using actual numbers?

"I know in your State of the Company meetings, Eileen and Vic have shared actual numbers on your V/TO. So, if you can recall some of that information from your last State of the Company, use that and tap into each other's brains to work your way down these five lines.

	20xx	%
SALES		100%
COGS		
GROSS PROFIT		
OPERATING EXPENSES		
NET PROFIT (BEFORE TAX)		

"Basically, I split the expenses into two buckets, which creates two kinds of profit. Let me explain. At the top of the income statement, we have Sales. Below that, we have Direct Expenses, like what Kristina was talking about. These are the expenses that are directly related to delivering your service. When you subtract your direct expenses from your sales, you get a number called Gross Profit. You'll do that math to get to a gross profit line and then take a guess at what you think your indirect expenses are. Some companies call these SG&A, or selling, general, and administrative expenses. What kind of expenses would you guess are in indirect costs?" asked Eddie.

"Insurance," said someone from the back of the room.

Another employee piped up. "What about utilities or building expenses like rent and office furniture?"

"Good," said Eddie. "What else?"

"Salaries for those of us who don't fall into direct expenses," said Kristina.

"Oh, that's excellent," said Eddie. "On your sheet, you'll fill in a guess for the indirect expenses, as well, and then subtract that number from the gross profit number. That will get you to the bottom line. The reason why I want to focus you on that net income line, which is sometimes called profit before tax, is because next year's incentive plan is going to be based on that bottom line."

Eddie gave the groups about ten minutes to brainstorm, talk, laugh, argue, arm wrestle, discuss, and debate. Each table had identified a scribe and had several copies of the blank income statement. They did their best work trying to guess the actual numbers for Swan Services' total year-end performance. The volume in the room increased with people laughing and arguing. Some groups were thinking quietly, and at the right time, Eddie said, "Two minutes left! Who needs more time?"

A few groups' hands went up, and all the teams kept talking.

A few minutes later, Eddie said, "Okay, let's come back together."

People started to quiet down, and the room became silent once again, with attention turned toward Eddie.

Eddie collected the final draft of the handout from each table. Each table had given their team a fun name, and Eddie said that the team closest to the actual numbers for this year would earn a gift card.

Eddie said, "I will share the actual answers soon, but first, I want to provide some context." He went through the Positive Tension curve and generated some conversation around tools that the Swan team was already using to create higher levels of performance. He shared the Adult Agreement, then talked about the benefits to Swan of everyone being open and honest and the importance of psychological safety. He helped the team understand the framework of moving from Me to We.

Everyone in the room seemed to be following and in agreement that "When we take better care of the company, we can take better care of ourselves."

As he got to the section called "Why bother," Eddie asked, "Why bother teaching employees about business and finance? Why bother helping you understand the bigger picture of how Swan makes money and how you add to or subtract value from the business with every decision you make every day? I can think of no better reason than this one: what your employees don't know can hurt you. What do I mean by that?

"Let me give you an example. I see this almost every week in different companies. Last week, I was meeting with a chemical manufacturer, doing some training with a group of front-line employees. I said to the group, 'Last year, your company did $20 million in sales. What percent of that do you think was profit?' One guy shoots his hand up and says, '65 percent.' Another guy raises his hand and says, '50 percent,' and so on. I heard the most amazing guesses, but the average I hear is about 50 percent.

"The reality at this company the prior year was that they hadn't made any money; they had actually lost money. The owner was mortified to hear his employees thought this. It was a real eye-opener.

"So, what's the problem if you have a group of employees walking around thinking the company makes 50 percent profit?" Eddie paused for answers.

"Where's my piece of that?" someone said.

"That's right. They think, 'Where's my piece of that?' Why else is it a problem if employees think the company is making 50 percent profit?"

"They might be more wasteful," said Evan.

"Right, more wasteful, and they may make assumptions. They think, 'So I wasted my time over there, or so I wasted that material—it doesn't matter because we're rolling in the money.' Only they don't say *we're* rolling in the money. Who do they say is rolling in the money?"

"The owner," said Melanie.

"That's right. The owner is 'rolling in the money.' Many employees think the owner is taking all the profit. What this can lead to, of course, is an 'Us vs. Them' mentality, and there can be real bitterness and mistrust there.

WHAT YOUR EMPLOYEES
DON'T KNOW
CAN HURT YOU.

"In the absence of information, people make up their own story. If we don't share information about how the company makes money or how small the profit really is, employees are going to believe what they want to believe. The rumors then become the truth because the company has not shared anything to the contrary," Eddie warned.

"But you shouldn't just start sharing financial statements and expect employees to suddenly understand and use this information to drive change in your company. It's important to realize that the purpose of sharing financial information with employees is not to make them into accountants. The purpose is to give them an educational basis for understanding why they should care. As I said earlier, most employees have the capacity and the interest. We just have to do it in a way that is non-threatening.

"Once you begin to see the big picture, we can tie additional tools you already use, like Scorecards, measurables, Level 10 Meetings, and Rocks, to help you better connect the dots and become more active in finding the money to fund the incentive plan.

"I have often been asked why more companies don't share information with employees. In my experience, the biggest reason is fear: fear that competitors will get a hold of the information or fear that customers will use the information to beat you up on price. But what are they going to do with it? Probably nothing. Our competitors are in the same industry we are in. Our margins are probably really similar. The reality is, though, we tell the employees that we don't share this information outside the company. We protect the company, just like we discussed with the Adult Agreement. Adults protect their homes and their families, and in this case, that's the company—our tribe.

"That leads us to the next question: How do you do it? Finance can seem pretty complicated to someone who has never been exposed to it, and trying something new can always be intimidating. I have found that the best way to teach finance to non-financial people is to relate it to something they know. I use a lot of comparisons to personal and household finance. When you tie personal finance to business, it makes it more relevant. What happens at home is very similar to what happens in business. So, we'll do that here today. I like to use pictures to help employees understand." Eddie began drawing on the whiteboard. "I used to do a bit of art in high school a long time ago; forgive me for these pictures." Eddie laughed.

He drew a small still camera at the bottom and wrote *Balance Sheet* next to it. He also drew what looked like a video camera. Next to that picture, he wrote *Income Statement* and *Cash Flow*.

"All companies use three financial statements to keep score for the company," Eddie said as he turned away from the whiteboard. "They use an Income Statement, a Cash Flow Statement, and a Balance Sheet. Now let me ask you this: What are these graphics telling us about these three statements?"

"The first two statements are moving, and the third is a snapshot in time," Melanie answered.

"Yes, two are dynamic, here, the Income Statement and Cash Flow Statement, versus this one, which is what?"

"A snapshot," Kristina called out.

"Right, and when you look at one snapshot compared to the next, what is the goal? What do you hope has happened?"

"That it has improved," Suzy said.

"Yes! When you boil it all down, each of these financial statements has three basic components, so let's talk about them.

"When you were in your small groups, we talked about the income statement. Although we talked about it having five lines, when you look at an income statement in its most detailed form, it can be many pages long. As I said when we started, an income statement is essentially three things. It's Sales minus Expenses equals Profit." He pointed to what he had written on the whiteboard.

$$SALES$$
$$-\ EXPENSES$$
$$\overline{PROFIT}$$

"Okay, now let's talk about cash. Cash is just three things as well. What happens to cash in your household?" he asked.

"My husband spends it!" Melanie called out.

Everyone laughed.

As the laughter subsided, Eddie said, "That's right, cash goes out. But before it goes out, it has to come in, right?"

Underneath Cash Flow, he wrote Cash In. Below that he wrote Cash Out and drew a line underneath the words Cash Out. "The difference is called the Change in Cash," said Eddie. "If you have more cash coming in than going out, then you have positive cash flow. Of course, if you have more cash going out than coming in, that's called negative cash flow, and that can be a problem, right?"

Everyone could see that *Sales* and *Cash In* were on the same line, and *Expenses* and *Cash Out* were on the same line. The results were that *Profit* and *Change in Cash* were on the same line, too.

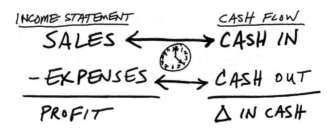

Eddie said, "From these two statements, you can tell that Profit is not the same thing as Cash. Is it possible to be profitable and run out of cash?"

"Absolutely!" said Vic.

"So, these two financial statements are related but different, correct?" Eddie asked.

Everyone nodded.

"What's the difference, in its simplest form?" Eddie posited.

"AR," said Jeff abruptly.

"Tell me more about that," said Eddie.

"AR stands for Accounts Receivable," said Jeff. "That number is the total cash our clients owe Swan. It's not the same as profit, though."

"That's great," said Eddie. "If you had to reduce it to one word, how could you describe the difference between cash and profit?"

"I suppose it would be timing," said Jeff.

"Perfect," said Eddie. "Timing is the difference. For example, just because we make a sale doesn't mean we have the cash, right? There is a timing difference, but we can manage that timing to our benefit. And we can manage how quickly we pay our vendors or how fast cash goes out. We can manage the timing of how quickly we collect our cash from our clients. It's important to point out that everyone can help with this—it's not just accounting. We want everyone to understand how they impact cash, and then we can all work together to improve cash flow."

Eddie paused. "One question for you: If our customers have our cash, who doesn't have it?"

"We don't!" said Evan.

Eddie replied, "That's right. And if we don't have cash, but we need cash for something, what might we have to do?"

"Borrow money," said Eileen.

"Yes, and when we borrow money, what's a new expense that we have to add to our income statement?" asked Eddie.

"Interest," said Kristina. "An interest expense."

"Yes," said Eddie. He drew arrows from *Sales* to *Cash In* and *Expenses* to *Cash Out*. He also drew an arrow from *Cash Out* back to *Expenses*. "So, cash goes out to pay some of our expenses. What are these expenses? You guys mentioned a few of them earlier: wages, rent, insurance, maybe interest if we borrow some money, and so forth. Just like at home, here at Swan Services, there are plenty of expenses, too. You can clearly see the relationship between cash and profit. From a financial statement standpoint, of course, we want both of these to be healthy.

"Let's talk about this third statement called a balance sheet. The balance sheet is three things as well. It's what you own," Eddie wrote the word *Own* to the left side and then an =, "which is what you owe, plus what you really own.

"Now, to keep it simple, let's compare it to a house. How many folks in here own a house?"

A few people raised their hands.

"Great," said Eddie. "So let's say you own a house." He drew a picture of a simple house with two windows underneath the word *Own.* "Do you really own the house?" asked Eddie.

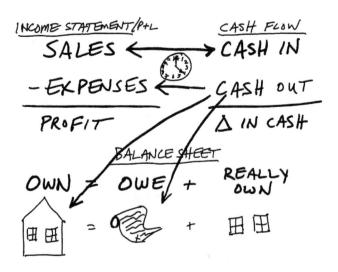

Someone shouted out, "No! I've got a mortgage."

"That's right," said Eddie, "and your mortgage is essentially debt. He drew a picture of a scrolled document that looked like a signed contract underneath the word *Owe.* "So maybe what you really own are the two windows on the house."

Everyone laughed as Eddie drew two windows under the words *Really Own.*

"That's essentially what a balance sheet is. There's more complicated terminology for this, like assets and liabilities and equity, but the essence of it is it needs to balance." Eddie said, "You've heard the phrase 'Cash is King'. Cash connects these three statements together. These arrows show that we use cash to pay our expenses, which shows up on the income statement. And also, we might use cash to invest in new assets, like new software, technology, or equipment at Swan."

He drew an arrow from *Cash Out* to *Own*.

"These are longer-term investments that ideally will lead to improving operational efficiencies or adding value for our clients through new or improved products or services."

Eddie drew another arrow from *Cash Out* to *Owe*.

"Last, cash might go out to help us pay down debt. So, in connecting these three statements, you can see that Cash is truly king." Eddie grinned as he scanned the group to ensure everyone was tracking with him. "What speaks to you most about what I'm teaching here?"

He waited a bit for a brave volunteer to speak up.

Jeff started. "I like the idea that it's really this simple. And that each of us actually do the same things at home. We have to manage our expenses, and we also might invest here or there."

"That's great, Jeff," Eddie said. "You're exactly right. When we compare business finance to personal finance, it does make it easier to understand."

Suzy raised her hand and asked, "If we buy something, like a new piece of expensive software for Swan, how does that impact our incentive plan?"

"Wow, that's a great question," said Eddie. "And you're a little ahead of me. But the short answer is 'it depends.' It will depend on how you decide to pay for that investment. For example, let's say the software costs $100K, and we use $50K of cash and borrow $50K from the bank. Now we have this $100K software. It's an asset. Something we own. Have we touched anything on the income statement at this point?"

Some people shook their heads.

"No, we didn't, not in the first month. Now, in subsequent months, we have a couple of new expenses. The first one we can associate with what happens when you buy a new car. When you buy a new car, let's say you go out and buy a new SUV. What happens to the value of that SUV over time?"

"It depreciates," said Jeff.

"Right. Depreciation is chunked into months over the life of the SUV, which is an expense, a non-cash expense. And when you borrow money, you have a new expense called . . ."

"Interest!" said a few in unison.

"Right, we have interest, which is an expense, of course, and when expenses go up, profit goes down. But then we ask the question, why did we buy this new piece of software?"

"To make us more efficient," said Kristina.

"Exactly," said Eddie. "As it relates to Suzy's question, we use the income statement to calculate the incentive plan. The idea is, as long as it's a good investment, the operational efficiencies we gain at Swan through the software should more than offset any new expenses we have of interest, depreciation, installation, training, and so forth. And that's why investments always carry with them some level of risk. If the return isn't there to compensate for the risk taken, then we should really question whether or not we should make the investment in the first place. Most teams also look at how long it takes for an investment to pay for itself. But that's a topic for another day. We can take a deep dive into that sometime and have more detailed conversations on how capital investment works. Bottom line is that the risk-return equation is a really important concept. Thank you so much for asking that question, Suzy."

Eddie paused to let the moment pass. Finally, he said, "Let's go back to this income statement for a second. I'm sure you're all curious as to how you did on the blank income statement exercise. You guys want to see the real answers?"

Everyone was energized to see the answers. Eddie clicked to the next slide. It showed a simple income statement that reflected $8 million at the top line, a 49 percent gross margin, and 10 percent at the bottom line.

There were groans and shouts of disbelief coming from the group. Some people laughed, and the table to Eddie's left high-fived each other.

"Looks like we may have a winner-winner chicken dinner!" said Eddie. "Let's look at your guesses. Table Grey Goose—great name, by the way—wrote a bottom line of 20 percent. Not a bad guess, but you're a bit high.

"Table Swan Lake . . . I'm seeing a theme here."

Everyone was laughing.

"18 percent.

"The Fabulous Thunderbirds: 25 percent; Chicken Littles: 10 percent. Excellent!" Eddie put that one to the side.

"Team Gorilla Panic: 15 percent; and The Mudhens, also 15 percent. So, Team Chicken Littles is our winner!"

Smiling, Eileen walked to the winning table and handed each team member a gift card.

Eddie explained, "These gift cards are for having the most accurate guess on profit for this year. If you think of it in terms of $1 in sales and a 10 percent profit, you can see that Swan Services is keeping a dime on the dollar. And that's before taxes. It's also before reinvestment, servicing any debt, and providing a return on investment to the people taking all the risk.

"Now, I want to show you some historical financial trends for the organization from the last several years and ask you to reflect on what you see going on with these trends."

Eddie flipped through some specific Swan Services financial trends and charts, looking at revenue, revenue per employee, gross margin, gross margin percent trends, as well as trends in the profit line—which showed a steady increase in bottom-line profitability over the last few years.

"What's interesting to consider from my perspective is the hockey stick nature of the profitability curve as well as the revenue curve. Consider when you began implementing EOS," said Eddie. It was clear from the charts that the company's financial performance had increased steadily beginning the year after they implemented EOS.

Eddie also talked about how Swan's financial performance compared to industry standards, pointing out that industry standards are average and that Swan wants to be exceptional. "I see a lot of amazing things happen at companies when everyone knows where to look."

Eileen approached Eddie at the front of the room as they had agreed. Eddie said, "I'm going to turn over the mic to Eileen, who's going to help us facilitate this group activity. Thank you so much for your time, participation, and energy. I'm really excited about what Swan has in store for you over the coming years. I have no doubt that what you are targeting on that V/TO is absolutely attainable if you continue to stay laser-focused on keeping it simple and holding each other accountable using the Adult Agreement. Thank you!" said Eddie.

The Swan team gave Eddie an energetic round of applause.

Eileen said, "Thank you, Eddie! Alright, everyone, we're going to take a quick break. When we return, we're going to not only talk about the incentive plan for next year, but we'll also discuss ways that we as a team can drive improved profitability to help us fund that incentive plan and create job security and opportunities for all of us."

After the break, Eileen shared the final version of next year's incentive plan with the group. It was simple, on one slide, and easy to explain to the group. She talked about the philosophy behind a profit trigger, the concept of the incentive plan being self-funded, and that the payout frequency would be quarterly with a holdback.

She also shared that she and Vic were committed to keeping the same plan in place throughout the year even if they were blowing the doors off the place, and also that they wouldn't be paying an incentive if they didn't surpass the trigger.

Eileen then changed gears and set up a group activity so the team could think about ways to increase operational efficiencies as well as capitalize on growth opportunities. "The next exercise is called the Leaky Pail Exercise. To kick off this exercise the right way, I want to take a step back and talk about personal finance. One of the things Eddie shared with us is that one of the easiest ways to teach business finance is to compare it to something with which we're all familiar: personal finance.

"Vic and I really believe that the lessons we are teaching you about the business will help you better manage your personal finances, as well."

Eileen navigated to a slide that showed a personal income statement example. "Let's say you're somebody who takes home $2,200 a month, and you spend your money in this way at home," she said, pointing to the left-hand side of the slide. "You've got your mortgage, your cell phone bill, your food expenses, and utilities. At the end of the month, you've got 100 bucks left.

"Let's say you're not satisfied with that. You decide to get smart and do some things differently. Every single one of these things we do at home, we want to associate with something we could do at Swan.

YOUR PERSONAL FINANCES

MONTHLY INCOME	$2,200	MONTHLY INCOME	$2,200
MORTGAGE	$1,000	REFINANCE MORT.	$900
PHONE BILL	$125	CHANGE PHONE CO.	$75
FOOD	$400	FOOD BUDGET	$350
UTILITIES	$200	CONSERVE UTILITIES	$125
CAR EXPENSE	$175	CAR MAINTENANCE	$125
CREDIT CARDS	$200	PAY DOWN CCs	$225
PROFIT	$100	VACATION FUND	$100
		HOME IMPROVEMENT	$100
		PROFIT	$200

"In this example, maybe this person refinances his mortgage to save a little money. When you refinance your mortgage, what are you actually doing?"

"You're reducing your interest expense," said Todd.

"Yes, and what is something we might do at the company that would be equivalent to refinancing your mortgage at home?"

"Maybe restructure our debt?" Sue answered.

"That's right, maybe we could get a better interest rate by restructuring our debt. Thankfully, we don't have a lot of debt here at Swan," Eileen said with a smile and returned to the example. "This guy decides to change his cell phone provider to save a little money on his monthly phone bill. What might be something similar in our business to changing a phone provider?"

"Same thing," called out Evan.

"Exactly. Same thing. We could re-examine *all* of our vendor relationships in a broader scope. We could go out and change things instead of sticking with what we know.

"Now, this person is going to go on a food budget. Maybe he doesn't go out to eat as much. He shops at Sam's Club or Costco instead of Whole Foods. What would be equivalent at Swan?" Eileen paused. When nobody spoke up, she suggested, "How about managing our controllable expenses like office supplies, postage, or other small administrative expenses?"

The crowd nodded in unison.

"Our hero here is able to conserve utilities and reduce his subscriptions, which lowers his monthly bills. He takes better care of his car, which results in lower repair costs, less downtime, better fuel efficiency, and so forth. What would that be in our business?"

"Same thing," said Kristina. "Taking care of our equipment, the building, and so forth."

"Right. Next, he pays down credit cards. Now, by doing some things a little smarter, he's got a bunch of money he didn't have before. The first thing he's going to do is to pay down some debt. What happens when you pay down debt? Lower interest payments, right? He also started putting some money away in a vacation fund: $1,200 a year. What would that be at Swan?" Eileen asked rhetorically. Then she answered, "That's our incentive plan; it's been self-funded through the changes we made in our expenses.

"Our guy also found $100 a month to put back into his home. What's that going to do to the value of his home?"

"It's going to increase it," Evan called out.

"Yes, and it's the same thing in our business," Eileen replied. "At the end of the month, he has some money left over. He's the shareholder—he can keep that. In your business, that's retained earnings—same thing.

"Alright," Eileen continued, "that's the setup. Let's do an exercise together. It has to do with finding the money falling through the cracks in the pail. Let's imagine a pail that represents our business. All the water in the pail is your revenue. During the month, the revenue is getting smaller and smaller because we have these expenses running through the business. There is direct labor, salaries, office supplies and other administrative costs, insurance, rent, utilities, etc. The water is sloshing out and being scooped out, and this is what's left over: this is profit. But it's a leaky pail. As we keep saying, there are a bunch of cracks in the pail, and we can put those cracks into two categories.

"One is inefficiencies. These are things like rework, wasted time, errors, overtime, and so forth. You and I both know a company can't become the best in class by focusing its energy on cutting costs. So, what else is there?"

This was another rhetorical question, but Eileen paused to allow everyone to process it. "Missed opportunities.

For businesses like ours, it could be new products, new services, new technologies, new strategic alliances, or new market territories. If we miss those opportunities, those are cracks in the pail as well.

"To get us all thinking about this, let's get back into our small groups. Partner up, feel free to move chairs, and make sure you're in groups of 3 or 4 people. Once you have your group, figure out who has the best handwriting. That person can be the scribe. They'll take notes on the ideas you come up with. Remember, we're brainstorming! There are no wrong answers!" Eileen shouted as everyone formed their groups.

The volume picked up as people talked and moved their chairs together. Immediately, the small groups were busy laughing, talking, and brainstorming.

Wow, she thought. *This is really working!*

"Find the cracks in the pail," Eileen reminded them as she walked around the room, "and remember the Adult Agreement: just say it! There are no wrong answers. Adults don't shoot each other's ideas down."

After about ten minutes, Eileen called the group back together and settled everyone down. "Alright, let's go around and get one idea from each group. I'll write them on this flip chart up here. Scribes, look at your list and take your best shot. What's going to have the greatest impact in the shortest amount of time?"

She heard one idea from each group, then went around the room again, building a list of nearly 20 ideas on the flip chart. Training, labor efficiency, waiting on the customer, supplies, utilities, work smarter . . . the list on the flip chart continued to grow.

After she had exhausted the groups' ideas, she asked, "Wow, how much money do you think is in these ideas?"

Several people guessed—the range of guesses was anywhere from $100K up to $500K.

"Great estimates! Now, here's a question: How much would our sales have to increase to put $500K to the bottom line if we do 10 percent profit at Swan?"

Eileen paused a beat to let the question sink in. She could see the team thinking and perhaps doing some mental math.

"An easy way to do this is to divide that number—let's take $500K as an example for easy math—by a profit of 10 percent, or .1. And we can see how much more we'd have to sell to make this much profit. If we do that math, we can see that 500,000 divided by .1 equals 5 million dollars.

"Now, that's certainly a guesstimate to illustrate the math, but wow," Eileen said. "I have no doubt we can fund our incentive plan with ideas like this. It's just about all of us becoming more aware of these things and their impact on our business. Doing things a little differently can have a huge impact on our profit and our incentive plan." She ripped off the flip chart sheets and emphatically stuck them to the conference room wall.

"OK, so we're done with this exercise. A lot of this is about awareness, and hopefully, we are thinking a little differently now."

Eileen continued facilitating and teaching the team as she had rehearsed. Before they concluded the meeting, she brought the conversation around to the next steps and let them know that she and Vic would be sharing Swan Services' financial updates quarterly and that as ideas or concerns occurred to anyone at any time, they should add those to their departmental issues lists so those issues could be prioritized and addressed.

CHAPTER 9

TENSION TOOLS

As Swan Services got through the first quarter of the new year and were able to close their books, Jeff calculated that they had surpassed the trigger for that quarter and generated a small payout in the incentive plan. They adhered to the simple payout formula they had designed, banking 50 percent of the first quarter's total incentive pool to the end of the year and planned to pay out the remaining 50 percent.

As they prepared for Swan's State of the Company Meeting, Eileen spent time watching the videos in Eddie's online ProfitLink Masterclass and preparing herself to not only share the year-to-date score with everyone but also to teach a few more business and finance concepts.

After talking with Eddie in her quarterly coaching call, she and Vic decided they would re-teach the income statement at the first quarter's State of the Company Meeting to keep it fresh. They also wanted to talk about cash and the difference between profit and cash.

Jeff brought to Eileen's attention that Accounts Receivable (AR) had begun creeping up, and he thought it might be a good idea to talk to the group about collections and cash.

Eileen asked Jeff to take the lead on teaching that part and helped him log into the ProfitLink Masterclass video library to prepare a group activity about cash.

Since the slides and handouts were 80 percent completed, this was an easy task. Jeff downloaded the slides and handouts, added the Swan logo to the slides, and changed a few of the numbers to reflect Swan's actuals. To prepare, Jeff watched a short video a few times that showed him how to teach and facilitate the exercise. He also printed worksheets for everyone in preparation for the meeting the following week.

The next week, it was an early start. As the group assembled for the first State of the Company Meeting, there was excitement in the air. Everyone wanted to hear how Swan was progressing toward their annual plan. Eileen had arranged a breakfast buffet for the team and planned to get everyone out by 7:30 am so they could have a productive day.

As the group was gathering, Eileen noticed there was not much talk about the incentive plan, perhaps because everyone was so used to receiving it at the end of the year.

"As you guys know," Vic said as he began the meeting, "we hold this meeting each quarter to keep you up to speed on where we've been, where we are, and where we're going. This is a particularly special meeting as it's the first one where we'll also be talking about our progress on this year's self-funded incentive plan.

"Using Eddie's advice, each quarter, we will teach a simple business education or financial literacy exercise to keep reinforcing the content for all of us about what profit is and how it is generated at Swan. I don't know about you guys, but when I don't see this information for a long enough time, I need a little reminder because it's not something I look at every day."

Vic walked through the last 90 days at Swan, high-lighting a few new hires, some new "whales" (projects over $100K that they signed that quarter), as well as reviewing their year-to-date financials against the budget.

"As you can see," Vic pointed out, "we surpassed our profit trigger this quarter, which means we will have a first-quarter payout."

Everyone clapped as Vic continued. "Well, don't get too excited yet. Even though we're ahead, we'll need to maintain this pace to stay ahead of the game throughout the year.

"I want to share with you some details for a few projects that wrapped up at Swan this past quarter. Take a look at this chart," Vic said as he motioned to the projected slide. "This is data about our Crimson Supplies project. We started the new ERP implementation with them early last year. This was the budget in terms of sales and gross margin."

Vic was sharing a bar chart slide with the group. "As you can see," said Vic, "we had budgeted a 50 percent gross profit, which I'll remind you is after we pay all of our direct costs for that project: labor and materials.

"Now check this out," said Vic. He advanced the slide, and the actual labor costs, material costs, and gross profit appeared on the slide next to the budget. "As you can see, Crimson Supplies was a home run. We exceeded our gross profit target by over $13,000, which is not insignificant."

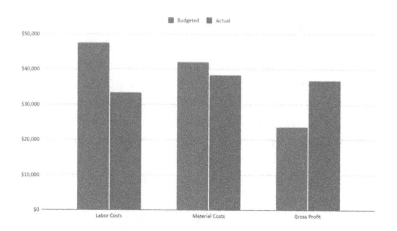

There were some whistles and a few claps as Vic asked, "Show of hands, who worked on the Crimson project?"

Several hands went up around the room, and Vic said, "Let's give these guys a round of applause."

The room exploded with hoots, hollers, and thundering applause.

Vic said, "Hey, Shep, would you mind telling us a little bit about what you guys did to manage the labor on this project so effectively?"

Shepherd stood up and said, "I'll tell you what, Vic. This is new to us, but having access to timely, accurate data each week allowed us to pivot and allocate labor properly when we were getting ahead of the client or if we were falling behind a little bit. We also started having weekly huddles that were exclusively focused on Crimson Supplies issues. These huddles included a Crimson Supplies Scorecard with measurables specific to this project. I think that really helped us with the frequency of the communication and 'stepping on dinosaur eggs before they turned into dragons,' so to speak."

Everyone laughed at Shep's analogy, and then he continued. "I can't thank the group enough for their hard work, tireless effort, and for bringing attention to issues early. That really helped us stay ahead in terms of the profitability of the project."

"Thank you, Shep," said Vic. He paused to transition to the next topic.

"Now, I also want to share with you all a project that we'll affectionately call a "train wreck." This is one we've all known about because it's been about two-and-a-half years that we've been working on this other ERP implementation. Even though we're behind budget on this project, the good news is that by using some of the habits Shep mentioned for this project, Anil has been able to stabilize the margin erosion.

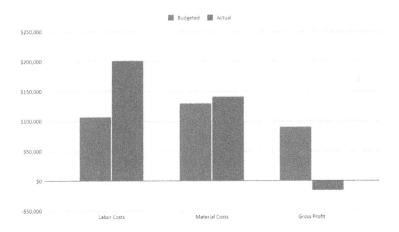

"As you can see from this chart, the team is managing overtime in a smart way, and they have also added a few additional profitable services to the project that the client needed but that we hadn't scoped prior to the project. All these efforts are helping us put a tourniquet on and stop the bleeding," Vic explained.

"Anil, I don't want to put you on the spot, and I want you to know that this isn't a blame game, but would you be open to saying a few words about how this project is wrapping up?" As Vic spoke, he was conscious of keeping Eddie's points about psychological safety in mind.

Anil said, "Sure, thanks, Vic. I know this is a team effort, and the group is super tuned in to the numbers now, especially because we see such a direct link between these gross margin dollars and the potential payout in our incentive plan. What I plan to do as the project wraps up this next quarter is to put together a document that is somewhat of a postmortem reflection on what went well and what we would have done differently knowing what we know now. Perhaps what I can do is share that with everyone at Swan and maybe summarize it at our next State of the Company meeting?"

"Excellent idea. That would be great," said Vic. "Eileen, will you make a note about that? Thank you, Anil."

Vic advanced slides. He walked the team through where Swan is today, then began talking about the Vision side of the V/TO.

They did some core values shoutouts, during which there were lots of laughing and high fives.

As the team started to settle back into their seats again, Vic asked, "Eileen, do you wanna take it from here and talk a little bit about the Traction side of the V/TO?"

Eileen went to the front of the room and started to walk through the 1-Year Plan, reinforcing the numbers they had agreed on for the budget and their four goals for the year. They had added the measurables Gross Margin and Net Profit to the V/TO on both the 3-Year Picture™ and the 1-Year Plan as well as underneath the Rocks section on the Traction side of the V/TO.

"As you can see, we've added a few measurables to our V/TO to stay in alignment with our new incentive plan and keep you all up to speed on knowing the score as we're playing the game, not just at the end of the game."

They talked about the first quarter's performance, the new Company Rocks for the quarter, and shared the year-to-date income statement. There was a great discussion about how the departmental Scorecards tied into the company's year-to-date income statement.

Eileen said, "One thing we've noticed as we've started really tuning into the connection between departmental Scorecards and the company's year-to-date income statement is that a few of our larger clients are taking longer to pay us. There's a measurable called Average Collection Days that I'm going to ask Jeff to talk about, and we'll do a short exercise so that we're all on the same page with the impact of these payment delays on our ability to grow."

Jeff said, "Thank you, Eileen. Eddie asked us a question last year that was pretty simple, but it made it very clear how cash works. He asked us, 'If our customers have our cash, who doesn't have it?' And, of course, the answer is, 'We don't.' We don't want to get to the end of a quarter and not have any money to pay our incentive, let alone all the other problems that can cause. Of course, we're not going to borrow money to pay bonuses, I mean incentives.

"As you can see from this slide, it takes us, on average, about 58 days to collect our money," Jeff said as he looked out at his peers. "Basically, that means that our clients pay us, on average, 58 days from the date of the invoice. Now, most of our clients have terms that are net 30, and a few of our larger clients have negotiated more favorable terms for themselves. Advanced Electronics, for example, negotiated net 60 as their terms, meaning they'll pay us 60 days from the date of the invoice. That's not unusual, and it will drag up our average, but if we pull out several outliers like that, we can see that a few of our clients who have net 30 terms are stretching those out.

"A question for you," said Jeff. "What are some of the reasons that our clients don't pay us on time?"

The room was silent for a moment while people thought through the question. Melanie raised her hand and said, "Maybe the invoice is wrong?"

"That's possible, Melanie," said Jeff. "And if we see invoice accuracy issues, let's all agree to add those to an issues list wherever it comes up. What are some other reasons people don't pay bills on time? Even you or me."

"Maybe they don't have the money?" asked Kevin.

"Good point, Kevin", said Jeff. "And although that may be true, we don't want their cash flow challenges to become our problem. We would definitely want to add that to an issues list early if anyone sees that happening at a client.

"Other thoughts on why our customers don't pay us on time?"

"If I'm not happy with the service or the product, I might not be that psyched to pay it so quickly," said Shep.

"That's good," said Jeff, "and maybe that's why these clients are delaying payment, but as Eddie pointed out last year, this isn't just an accounting issue; this is a Swan issue. We all need to stay tuned in to our customers' payment habits because often when we're on-site with these projects, we can put in a good word, help our invoice get to the top of the pile, or otherwise make it easier for our clients to pay us. What I propose is that in our project huddles with each of our technology projects, especially the big ones, we should add a measurable for each project around the open AR dollars and their age. That will help us bring awareness to the issue, and then if an invoice becomes egregiously past due, we can pop it on an Issues List and identify what the solution will be."

Eileen jotted down Jeff's idea as an issue for their next leadership team meeting.

"I'd like to show you a simple example of the impact it would have on Swan if we reduced our average collection days from 58 to, say, 45, a reduction of 13 days. If we take our monthly sales, which is a little shy of $1,000,000 and divide it by 30 days, we get our average daily sales. We take that number and multiply it by 13 days' improvement. You can see it's about $350,000."

"Wow," said a few from the audience.

"Think about that," said Jeff. "What could we do with $350,000? Buy new equipment, hire more people, put together a marketing campaign . . . . If we could improve collections by 13 days and speed up the collection of these dollars that our customers owe us, we could pay down debt, start a new business, pay the bonus—you get the picture. We can invest it sooner to create more growth in our organization. Also, if we improve it, another risk we minimize is the potential for that increasing AR to become bad debt, which can happen if we take our eyes off the ball.

"Then, the real question becomes: How do we reduce average collection days? Here's what I'd like to do: I'd like you to get in groups of three or four and talk for a couple of minutes about cash, payment terms, and everything else related to this part of our process. I'd like each group to come up with your best idea for some tangible actions we can consider implementing as soon as next week. Sound good?"

Everyone nodded.

Jeff said, "Great, let's get into small groups, and I'll put ten minutes on the clock."

The groups discussed why customers don't pay in 30 days. They knew it could be a lot of reasons: customer service, quality, delivery, projects are late, they didn't understand the terms, we didn't ask them, the invoice was wrong, they didn't get the invoice, there's no advantage to paying early, and the idea of offering a cash discount.

Jeff captured the ideas on a list. He let the group know that he and his team would take these ideas to his department's Issues List, put together a game plan, and then let the team know their top three recommendations.

At the end of the exercise, Jeff turned the mic back over to Vic and Eileen. They advanced the slides to talk about the progress of the incentive plan.

They had created quarterly triggers that aligned with the annual trigger. The data showed that they had surpassed their first quarter's trigger. They showed that they had divided that pool in half, reflecting the fact that half of the money would be banked to the end of the year, and the other half would be paid out in the next paycheck.

Vic and Eileen helped the team see that right now, they were winning the game. They pointed out that they were putting the money to work but that there was no guarantee it would continue. They would have to continue to surpass the quarterly triggers in order to stay ahead.

As they moved to wrap up the State of the Company Meeting right on time, Eileen was feeling confident about the clarity of the plan, about the transparency that they had engaged in with the numbers, and about the team really starting to grasp the concept of how critical their decisions were toward the impact on gross profit, especially. She knew she and Vic had established a formula for the incentive plan rather than leaving it as a discretionary end-of-year bonus.

As she and Vic were driving back to Swan that morning, she shared her thoughts with Vic.

Vic responded, "Eileen, I can't tell you how excited I am to feel that vibe of people really beginning to think and act like owners."

"Me too, Vic," said Eileen. "It's really exciting to know that they are as concerned about the business, or getting there at least, as we are."

"Maybe they'll share the insomnia that we have about Swan, too," laughed Vic.

Eileen laughed, too. "No doubt!"

"Hey, and I have to say, Kristina has been a real rock star for us, helping different folks understand more about gross profit this quarter," said Vic.

"Definitely," said Eileen. "I was glad she got a core value shout-out from Jeff."

• • •

Eileen decided to introduce the idea of a Challenge Rock at the next quarter's State of the Company Meeting. A few weeks prior to the off-site, she logged into the Masterclass, downloaded the Challenge Rock template, and watched the short video a few times. She thought about how, at their core, Challenge Rocks are pretty straightforward. It's just a matter of gamifying a measurable Rock.

For one Challenge Rock, she thought she could get everyone to rally around a certain measurable: the number of client projects signed that are greater than $100K. After getting her ideas straight, she shared them with Vic. "If we can get 10 or more Whales signed this quarter, it looks like we'll be trending toward 11 million in sales, with a profit of around 12 percent, assuming we keep managing our labor in a way that helps us stay north of a 50 percent gross margin."

Vic agreed that this was a great idea.

At the next quarter's State of the Company Meeting, Eileen introduced Challenge Rocks to the team.

"A Challenge Rock is essentially a fun, high-involvement tool to amplify and improve one of our measurables," Eileen said before she walked them through each part of the template, describing the what and the why of each section.

After splitting the group into teams, Eileen continued. "In your groups, you each have one of these templates. As we've done in the past, identify a scribe, someone who will document what your team comes up with, and work as a team to draft a Challenge Rock. Now, you can pick any measurable you want. It could be something from your departmental Scorecard. It could be an issue you've been wrestling with recently, either out in the field on a client project or backstage at Swan, perhaps related to a process issue. Please note: You want to make sure you know what 'done' looks like. It should be binary, so we know if we've won the Challenge or not."

Eileen continued. "Also, one other thing, if you look at the bottom right of the template, it says 'If We Win . . .'.

In this section, the idea is to brainstorm some sort of celebration with your group. Ideally, we want to celebrate as a company, even if it's just one department that has accomplished the Rock. So, it could be a cookout, or we hire a band and have a party, or we bring in a masseuse for the day, or whatever! Sky's the limit on how creative you get with that. The goal is certainly to have fun, but we also want to pair that with a focus on improving our financial performance. So, make sure you focus on a meaningful Rock."

She released the groups to begin creating their Challenge Rocks. The noise increased noticeably as the groups laughed and challenged each other with their ideas.

After about 10 minutes, Eileen pulled the groups back together and asked each group to present their Challenge Rock to the rest of the organization. Some groups had searched the web for images and created some pretty fun posters with creative names.

Eileen's team presented "Whale Hunting," where the celebration would be a company boat ride on a nearby lake with fishing, drinks, and hors d'oeuvres. The other groups presented their Challenge Rocks on measurables such as labor efficiency, error reduction, and add-on sales.

After much laughter and excitement, Eileen tried to settle everyone down. "Great," she said. "You guys rocked this exercise. We'll add Challenge Rock Next Steps to our leadership team Issues List and circle back with you guys shortly on the immediate next steps. So, if we do this," she continued.

"When we do it!" Suzy shouted.

"Right, right! When we do this, what's the payoff?" Eileen asked.

"The incentive plan!" said Todd.

"Well, it's certainly the incentive plan," Vic interjected. "But more importantly, we're setting ourselves up for a great year next year. We're planting seeds, and the potential for hitting our 10-Year Target is much higher as well."

"So cool," said Eileen. "So it certainly is about the money in the incentive plan—that's important—but it's also about teamwork, the engagement, and having some fun along the way."

Eileen and Vic concluded the meeting and released everyone back to their days.

• • •

Throughout the year, Swan Services continued with their departmental Level 10 Meetings. They continued to refine their departmental Scorecards as more relevant measurables became apparent in each department, especially as it related to driving gross margin. Measurables around labor efficiency, utilization, and billable hours became the topics of conversation around project profitability and project efficiency. The teams discussed ways to reduce wasted time, wasted trips, and other inefficiencies, especially around their processes. They also focused on improving communication while on the projects.

They had conversations about measurables in sales, operations, and finance, and how these departmental measurables, if monitored regularly on a weekly basis, actually become leading indicators for the company's lagging performance indicated on the income statement.

In the third quarter, Jeff introduced a Challenge Rock around reducing average collection days from 50 to 45. The team decided that the celebration for accomplishing that goal of 45 days would be to hire a local country music band and have a BBQ with the whole company in October.

Each State of the Company Meeting seemed to get richer and richer. There were business and financial conversations and discussions about ways to foster growth at Swan Services. These ideas came not just from the leadership team but from the entire organization. The Swan team members were really beginning to look at the business like an owner does. They were more excited by the 10-Year Target™ than they had ever been even though it seemed like a BHAG, that North Star of becoming a $25 million company with 50 Whales, didn't seem so unrealistic.

At each State of the Company Meeting, they discussed and reinforced the impact that achieving their goals would have on everyone at Swan. This evolution toward an ownership culture certainly provided a source of job security for everyone, no doubt. More than that, though, the growth in Swan over the years would provide new opportunities for personal and professional development for the employees at Swan.

The growth was also helping them take better care of themselves; they were making more money, and most importantly, especially to Vic and Eileen, the stable growth that they saw at Swan was a clear indication that the company was having a huge impact on the lives not only of their employees but also on the families of their employees. This positive change undoubtedly had rippled to their clients as well as the customers of their clients. All these lives would be enhanced through the technology projects that Swan was enabling. The vision expressed on the V/TO was now beginning to feel like a company vision, not just that of Vic and Eileen. The employees were truly starting to think and act like owners.

CHAPTER 10

EARNING MINDSET

Toward the end of the year, Vic and Eileen were having another Same Page Meeting.

"We've got that culture committee started. I think Sheila will rock that," said Eileen.

"Tell me about the culture committee again," said Vic.

"Basically, the committee is a small, cross-functional group that will be in charge of the Challenge Rocks. They'll make sure there is one happening at least every quarter and then plan the celebrations around those when they win. They'll also be in charge of making the posters and planning the monthly 'Lunch and Learns' for ongoing financial training for those who want it. They will plan our State of the Company Meetings going forward, which is a huge help to me. Planning those is not my highest and best use." Eileen grinned.

"That's fantastic," said Vic.

"The other thing they'll handle is the new Swan Services University," said Eileen. She knew this idea would take Vic by surprise, so she paused to let him take in the thought.

"What the heck is Swan Services University?" asked Vic.

"It's so cool, Vic. I know you're going to love it, and we need your visionary brain thinking about everything we can do to get the most out of it," she responded. "At its basic level, we've taken the content from Eddie's online ProfitLink Masterclass and opened it up to all Swan team-mates so they can take personal financial management and business finance classes if they're interested. Jeff has volunteered to head it up. The idea is that if our team takes really good care of themselves at home, they will be more productive at work, and vice versa," Eileen explained.

"I'd also like to talk with you at our next Same Page Meeting about the idea of bringing in a life coach for our team once per week. Anyone could sign up for an hour with the life coach. The coach would talk with them about their life dreams, their family, their personal goals, and so forth, helping them think through what they would need to do to actualize them, to bring those dreams to life."

Vic was silent. Eileen could tell he was thinking about everything she had shared.

As Vic reflected on the last few years since they had implemented the ProfitWorks Solution and the years before when they implemented EOS, their long, winding journey to this point moved him deeply.

Vic thought about his and Eileen's many entrepreneurial ventures together: their lawn care business, bike repair shop, and even their lemonade stand. He and Eileen made a great team, he knew. Although their relationship was strained at times, he was proud of their discipline around how they implemented EOS, talked to and respected each other, and helped enroll the employees in the vision. They were successfully teaching them about business and finance, about profit and cash. He felt like they had accomplished so much toward their goal of creating a great company with great people and great results. Their 10-Year Target of $25 million in revenue at a 20 percent net profit didn't seem so out of reach now. They were staying laser-focused on solving real problems using the right technology for their clients. Vic was very proud of the Swan team that he and Eileen had assembled and the results of the game they were playing.

Vic could see that what Eddie had said was true: People play games to have fun, and people play games to win. Making business into a game for the Swan Services team helped them not only feel like but also truly become critical players on the team, focused on one score. They had avoided becoming a siloed organization by keeping the lines of communication open across the company and also by designing an incentive plan that was based on the results of the mothership, not just departmental results. He and Eileen had given the team the tools, the training, and the resources to allow them to actively participate in driving improvements at Swan. In this way, each member of this family was able to take better care of themselves.

● ● ●

A few weeks later at her business roundtable meeting, Eileen refilled her cup of coffee, gave Miguel a quick wave, and walked over to John to see how he was doing.

"Hi, John," said Eileen. "How's the construction business?"

John looked even more intense than usual. "Hey, Eileen," he mumbled. "I've got to say, it's been a lot of sleepless nights. My business seems to have hit a ceiling, as you say."

"Did you ever end up talking with Alan?" she asked.

"Yeah, we talked, but I couldn't stomach his daily fee, so we decided to self-implement Traction," John admitted.

"Actually, *Traction* is the book," said Eileen. "EOS is the operating system. I'm just teasing," she smiled. "So, how is the self-implementation going? What's working well?"

As they discussed EOS, John shared that the crews in the field were making a lot of mistakes and had a lot of overtime. Eileen suggested that perhaps John would benefit from a conversation with Eddie.

John said, "I don't think my people are capable of understanding financial concepts, Eileen."

Eileen replied, "I'm not gonna try to talk you into that, John, but I will share with you that I had my doubts with some of the people at Swan as well. With some of the tools that Eddie taught us and the gentler approach we took to wading our way into the financial-sharing swimming pool, we almost, I suppose, gently tricked people into understanding business."

"That's interesting," said John, turning toward her. "What do you think was the most impactful part for the employees?"

Eileen thought for a minute, then said, "Well, before we started sharing a lot of information, most of the Swan employees thought that our profit was 50 percent, and they thought that that was the number that Vic and I took home as owners in the business.

"One thing we realized was that on our V/TO, we were sharing some really large numbers: $8 million in sales, and $10 million in sales, $25 million in sales ten years out. Those are huge numbers for people to take in. Without any context for them to understand that sales are very different from profits, those numbers created a story for our employees in their heads about what they thought Vic and I were taking home from the business. It set us up for a major mental barrier.

"But, as we've shared more information over the years, we've become more patient, helping the team understand how precious profit is. We've been able to help them see how much they benefit when we increase profits, not only through the self-funded incentive plan but also through growth opportunities, job security, and reinvestment. It's elevated our team's experience. It's almost like we're finally having adult conversations with our team because we're not hiding anything."

Eileen continued. "Vic and I realized that when we weren't sharing information with our team, they not only made up stories about us but also it wasn't a lot of fun. The open and honest nature of this new transparency, paired with business literacy and EOS, helps us feel like we're putting all of our cards on the table. We're not operating in a silo or a vacuum; we have the support of our team."

John was listening to Eileen's dreamy chatter, but he remained skeptical. Eileen could tell by his demeanor that John just didn't think about people or business the same way she and Vic did.

A new roundtable member named Mandy came over to John and Eileen.

"Hi, I'm Mandy Cox," she said. "Bill invited me as a guest to this roundtable, and I thought I would introduce myself. Sorry to interrupt."

"No problem," said Eileen. "I'm Eileen Sharp, and this is John Fredrickson. My company is Swan Services, and John's in construction."

"Nice to meet you, Mandy." John waved as he got up to leave. "Hey, I'm gonna grab another cup of coffee before we get settled."

After John walked away, Eileen turned her full attention to Mandy and said, "Mandy, tell me a little about your business."

Mandy shared that she had started implementing EOS with the guidance of Alan Roth six months ago and that it was going great.

"That's awesome," said Eileen. "Tell Alan that Eileen says hello when you see him next at your quarterly."

"I will," said Mandy. "Bill mentioned that you had implemented an incentive plan that seems to be really helping you at your company. He suggested I ask you about it, as my business partner and I are wrestling with the same thing."

"Oh, sure," said Eileen. "Here, let me give you Eddie Stevens's contact information. His company is called ProfitWorks; he helps entrepreneurs like us create a culture of employees who think and act like owners."

"That sounds like exactly what we're trying to do," said Mandy.

Eileen shared Eddie's contact information with Mandy. "If you decide to hire Eddie to help you design the incentive plan and teach your employees, please let me know if I can help along the way."

"Thank you," said Mandy.

They found their seats, and Bill began the meeting by introducing the speaker.

IMPLEMENTING THE PROFITWORKS SOLUTION

As difficult as it may seem to help your employees think and act like owners, it doesn't have to be complicated. As there are significant costs of inaction, I share three discoveries below that I hope will make it easier for you to take a shortcut to implementation. Additionally, I've included a few simple ideas for getting started on your path to creating a culture of employees who are engaged and actively participate in helping you achieve your vision.

THE COSTS OF ENTITLEMENT MENTALITY

The concept of the left side of the bell curve has been in my life for as long as I can remember. I grew up in a household where my parents had very high and very clear expectations of performance for my boisterous brothers and me, and they helped us strive to want that for ourselves.

There are many costs for an individual who remains entitled. For one, if we protect someone from failure, we rob them of their ability to grow. They miss the opportunity to become a strong, independent person. By protecting them from risk, we destroy their ability to develop self-esteem. People are rewarded with self-esteem and self-confidence by stretching themselves out of their comfort zone, for accomplishing something they didn't know they could. Confidence must be earned. Individuals benefit from learning to think creatively and solve their own problems. They also learn from failure as they explore their boundaries and limitations. If we continually rescue them, we impede their ability to grow.

In organizations like Swan Services, the costs of entitlement range from a loss of productivity to the absence of innovative thinking and creative problem-solving to the unwillingness to take risks. This is in addition to apathy, and that the burden of your company's success is heavily weighted on you and your leadership team. It has repeatedly been demonstrated that morale is highest, and people produce more and are most creative when there is some pressure to perform.

To make things even tougher, wherever entitlement exists in an organization, the culture usually codifies it, and leaders who are afraid of rocking the boat often perpetuate it. Thus, it can require a significant shock to your business, the motivation of a crisis, or an intervention to finally change things. Also, since moving out of entitlement requires risk-taking, it will always involve overcoming fear.

One of my coaches, Steve Chandler, who is fond of teaching in distinctions, talks about serving versus pleasing. In the short run, serving people by requiring that they earn what they receive is certainly harsher than simply giving it to them. But in the long run, serving people is the only way they can gain self-esteem and independence. The bottom line is that when people are not held accountable for performance levels, they don't perform. We must empower people by giving them responsibilities and hold them accountable for their actions. Only in this way can we engender the achievement, growth, and confidence necessary for maximum productivity.

As Eddie teaches in this book, psychological safety must exist with accountability to get people out of their comfort zones. Amy Edmondson, author and a professor of leadership, teaming, and organizational learning, teaches us that freely admitting mistakes helps people learn better so they can eliminate those mistakes the next time, thereby increasing performance. In order to develop a culture where freely admitting mistakes is acceptable without fear of retribution or consequence, your leaders must create psychological safety. If accountability exists without psychological safety, then people move to the right side of the curve toward fear. If psychological safety exists without accountability, then people stay in the comfort zone at the left side of the curve. Only when you balance psychological safety with a culture of accountability can the company create an earning culture—the top of the bell curve.

If you're familiar with Maslow's Hierarchy of Needs, you will no doubt recognize that the safety needs at the bottom of his pyramid are more me-focused. As you move up his hierarchy, through love and belonging, past self-esteem, achievement, celebration, and respect, to the top of his ladder, we find self-actualization and realizing one's true potential: "What we can be, we must be," says Maslow. For many, this can be frightening, causing them to avoid taking risks and retreat to their comfort zone. To be self-actualized, though, provides the opportunity to make a huge difference in the world through positively impacting others.

Similarly, at the bottom of Dave Logan's Tribal Leadership model is "Life Sucks," a me-focused victim mindset. At the top of his model is "Life is Great." Logan's model is also a journey from Me to We, from a place of fear where "it's about me," to a broader world about Love, Impact, and We.

This is squishy and uncomfortable stuff for many, but my experience is that this is what it's all about. Life is too short! And it's up to us as leaders to help our teams find their way out of apathy, out of entitlement and the comfort zone, and into a mindset of achievement, earning, and realizing one's full potential.

THREE DISCOVERIES

In the course of my experience working with entrepreneurs and their teams over the last few decades, three critical discoveries have occurred to me. I share these with you here in the hopes they provide a shortcut for you to implement this methodology. In their simplest form, they are:

1. Start with People
2. Transparency Is Tension
3. Celebration Increases Trust

DISCOVERY #1 - START WITH PEOPLE

When we first started ProfitWorks in 1996, EOS didn't exist. No one had defined a business operating system with such specific, simple, and impactful tools as Gino Wickman did with EOS. For the first 15 years of my work, before EOS, we were implementing these employee engagement tools with the assumption that our clients' leadership teams were aligned and disciplined and that they were healthy teams. We couldn't have been further from the truth! When EOS came into my life, it was like seeing the matrix: I saw the ones and the zeros. I thought to myself, *Why would we create an incentive plan for people who aren't the right people? How do we get people to align to a vision that hasn't been agreed upon or stated?* EOS and a system for managing human energy must come first.

All the tools and disciplines to effectively manage people are embedded in this operating system. The key is for you and your leadership team to get disciplined about using them. There needs to be more than an incentive plan to lead and manage your people. You and your RPRS (Right Person, Right Seat) leaders must do this hard work. And EOS provides the tools.

If discipline around people is weak in your organization, I suggest you start here. This is why the operating system and a holistic set of tools and disciplines must be in place first with a committed, aligned leadership team. With strong leaders in place who can have hard but compassionate conversations with people, holding them accountable and helping them move out of entitlement, you have a strong foundation to build this culture of earning. Great leaders must lead people out of entitlement via clear expectations, measurement, and feedback. Additionally, leaders must exhibit confident humility, as trust is enhanced when vulnerability exists.

Specific Actions:
1. Read *Traction* by Gino Wickman and *Get A Grip* by Gino Wickman and Mike Paton.
2. Find and hire a Professional EOS Implementer to help you run your business on EOS.

DISCOVERY #2 – TRANSPARENCY IS TENSION

My second discovery is that once you are on your way to having the right people in your organization, and they are in the right seats, you become open to some level of information sharing. Tied to my first discovery of starting with people, measuring performance and the visibility of measurables that goes along with this will help you create higher levels of accountability, which is a form of tension. It also helps you cascade the ownership of results deeper into your organization, which will help your leaders elevate as their teams bear more of the burden.

Assuming the right people are in place, transparency of information will create tension because your team will naturally be compelled to respond to that information, ideally taking action to improve the results, creating higher levels of expectations, visibility, and performance.

In the absence of information, people make up their own stories, and they will stay on the left side of the bell curve. Increasing transparency will increase trust, but keep in mind that transparency and providing more information to your people is a form of tension and higher expectations. So, with this transparency and increased accountability, be sure to exercise the Adult Agreement. It requires that people feel comfortable disagreeing and that disagreement doesn't have to be hostile. The Adult Agreement will help your team focus on developing superior solutions in an environment of psychological safety.

Specific Actions:
1. Fill out the free Mindset Scorecard to assess where you are with transparency and other mindsets. ProfitWorksLLC.com/ProfitWorks-Solution

2. Begin sharing more detailed financial information with your leadership team and set the expectation that they will become the company's champions to cascade this information (eventually) in your State of the Company Meetings as well as in departmental meetings. Provide context for the data by sharing more of the why behind the numbers.
3. Use the Adult Agreement. ProfitWorksLLC.com/Stretch-Not-Snap-Resources/

DISCOVERY #3 — CELEBRATION INCREASES TRUST

In "Trust Factor" by neuroscientist and author Paul Zak, he teaches us that ovation, which is defined as an enthusiastic show of appreciation and celebration, causes our brains to make and release the chemical oxytocin, which he calls the trust chemical. When this chemical is released, we feel the effects of celebration, motivation, and appreciation. The opposite would be to feel stress, worry, and fear.

The positive correlation between trust and celebration is my third discovery. Organizations that regularly incorporate celebration as part of their culture balance intrinsic and extrinsic rewards effectively. In these companies, I see more peer-to-peer recognition and core values callouts; I see teams that hug more, and I see teams that celebrate little wins frequently. All these behaviors lead to high trust, high performance cultures.

When pressure and the potential for failure are present, and teams succeed and then celebrate their success, they feel the pride of accomplishment. They feel intrinsic rewards like camaraderie and relatedness. The Challenge Rocks that Eddie teaches in this book are games, and when teams win games, they not only feel that same pride, but they also rest even briefly in a feeling of gain.

Increasing numbers of companies are giving employees full financial information and saying, 'If we reach a certain level of profitability, we get a reward.' They are sending the message that rewards are possible, but only if certain conditions are met; it won't be a gift. This tension sets your team up with clear expectations and balances that intrinsic feeling of pride and an earned reward with an extrinsic celebration of a financial payout that allows oxytocin and dopamine to flow.

Very simply, some amount of pay must be at risk when people are too comfortable. Of course, there are many kinds of rewards, not all of them financial. Being a member of a winning team or being publicly recognized are extremely important rewards, but money is an obvious one. I suggest some amount of money be at risk, but my passionate plea is not to view an incentive plan as a way to compensate for or subsidize a poor compensation structure. Fix this Me-comp issue first.

Specific Actions:
1. Celebrate an incentive plan payout and, when doing so, shine the spotlight also on the intrinsic reward—the grit, the teamwork, the effort—rather than just on the extrinsic dollars.
2. Introduce more ways to celebrate at your company. In State of the Company Meetings, publicly celebrate teams and individuals and encourage your teams to recognize each other. Encourage and model core values callouts.

GETTING STARTED WITH THE PROFITWORKS SOLUTION

The ProfitWorks Solution is a proven methodology for not only improving the financial performance of your firm but also positively changing its culture. Leaders running their businesses on EOS and committing to the principles outlined in this book can transform their companies in a very short time. It is truly incredible what your team can do when everyone knows where to look.

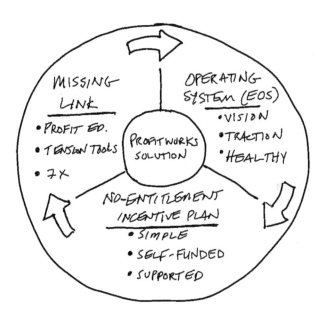

The Model itself is somewhat of a process. I suggest starting in the upper right of this model by implementing a business operating system (I'm biased toward EOS, of course). Once you are up and running for a few months on EOS and you are strengthening your leadership team alignment and your company's People Component, I suggest the following:

1. Read the book *Profit Works* and design and rollout a simple, self-funded incentive plan.
2. Sign up for the ProfitLink Masterclass, and begin teaching business acumen on a regular formal basis as a foundation first and roll out the incentive plan once this foundation has been established. (www.StretchNotSnap.com)

Changing the culture of one team is less daunting than changing the culture of an entire organization. So, when teaching business acumen, start with a team of internal champions, ideally your leadership team. When the whole organization needs to change, the driving force must be the top leaders. If you can build a coalition of champions committed to making a change and arm them with the tools you most likely already have in place, my experience is you will move farther faster. It has been repeatedly demonstrated that one of the best ways to learn is to teach. These internal champions can be incredibly effective at teaching their direct reports and integrating the tension tools that may already exist in your organization.

As we've said, only positive tension takes people and organizations out of entitlement. But tension is only half the prescription; the other half is support. Tension takes the form of required achievement, and support takes the form of information, coaching, and tools. Your leaders must be prepared to maintain and model positive tension, as well as to understand that their role is to support their teams and cascade this behavior. The benefit, of course, is that we develop leaders, who develop leaders, who develop leaders.

ACKNOWLEDGMENTS

I have more people than ever to thank for their support and assistance. There is no way to name you all individually because I would certainly leave someone off the list. Here's how I'm feeling.

So much gratitude certainly goes to my wonderful wife, Christine, for her patience, love, and strength, which I admire so much. You are my rock, sweet. Your big brain, your loving heart, your patience with my hyper-achiever, ADHD nature—I can never thank you enough. I am also grateful to our kids, Alec, Sophia, and Ethan. Mom and I are so proud of you all. Thank you for making our lives rich, rewarding, and full of laughter.

Special thanks go to my dear parents, Don and Betsy. Dad, your calm inspiration . . . the more I discover about all you have left behind, the more you blow my mind. Your big brain, your sense of humor, your eternal optimism. You remain a hero to me. Thank you. Mom, you were such a patient guide for Don, Gavin, and me. Your ability to instill discipline, get Dad to stay on the same page with you, and serve as an incredible role model for us . . . your impact can't be overstated. Thank you, Mom. I love you.

Don and Gavin, thank you both so much for being great role models for me. You both know I love you very much. Thank you for being great big brothers, great mentors, and for being great friends. I look forward to more time together.

I'm extremely grateful to Becky, Peter, and Christine for their loyalty, patience, and support. They are so much more to me than colleagues, and their commitment amazes me every day. Special thanks to Becky for keeping me organized and believing in me.

Thanks to my clients for your trust, openness, and hard work. You make me a better coach. I appreciate your faith in me and willingness to laugh with and at me. Thank you for your commitment to building cultures of employees who think and act like owners.

Thank you to all EOS implementers and the entire EOS Implementer Community. I can't thank you enough for all your support and for your belief in me and ProfitWorks. Thank you for trusting ProfitWorks to take care of your clients.

To the team at EOS Worldwide, especially Mark, Kelly, Amber, and Pam, for your passion, support, and belief in me. Thank you.

Thank you, Gino and Paton, for your advice, counsel, encouragement, and friendship. Thank you for challenging me on this sequel.

Thank you, Shannon Waller, and all my friends at Strategic Coach for helping me think about my thinking.

Thanks to my editors, Leslie Horn and Jill Ellis, and to all my test readers for helping me tighten up the manuscript.

And special thanks to my publisher, Kary, and to all the passionate people at Igniting Souls for their hard work and commitment. Thank you once again for blessing me with a fantastic title, Kary. I appreciate your creativity, professionalism, and for your help in getting this book to its final state. Kary suggested the title of this book. It was inspired by a phrase researcher and author Steven Kotler uses when he describes the concept of flow. He teaches that peak performers are most likely to get into a flow state when a challenge is just to the right of the challenge-skills sweet spot. When we're stretching but not snapping. It causes us to be laser-focused and stay in the zone, and this results in higher levels of performance. Thank you, Steven Kotler.

I am a big book reader if you can't tell. My number one strength on CliftonStrengths assessment is Input, meaning I crave to know more. Over the years, I have collected so much information not only from great books but also from the many managers, mentors, business partners, and coaches I have had. Thank you to all of you for sharing with me, teaching me, inspiring me, and believing in me. My journey to mastery is endless.

And thank you, Ayn Rand. "Who is John Galt?"

REFERENCES & SUGGESTED READING

Overcoming entitlement mentality and getting your vision shared by all are endlessly interesting topics that other authors have explored with great skill. I am inspired by work from each of the following 15 authors, and I encourage you to read the following books, which are listed in alphabetical order by title, for a deeper understanding of some of the concepts I discuss in *Stretch Not Snap*.

- *Atlas Shrugged*, Ayn Rand
- *Danger in the Comfort Zone*, Judith Bardwick
- *The Five Dysfunctions of a Team*, Patrick Lencioni
- *Flow: The Psychology of Optimal Experience*, Mihaly Csikszentmihalyi
- *Get A Grip*, Gino Wickman and Mike Paton
- *The Great Game of Business*, Jack Stack
- "Managing with the Brain in Mind," David Rock
- *On Becoming A Leader*, Warren Bennis
- *Ownership Thinking*, Brad Hams
- *Profit Works*, Alex Freytag and Tom Bouwer
- *Radical Candor*, Kim Scott
- *The Rise of Superman*, Steven Kotler
- *The Speed of Trust*, Stephen Covey
- *Traction*, Gino Wickman
- *Tribal Leadership*, Dave Logan

About the Author

Alex Freytag is the creator of ProfitWorks, a business coaching and training company focused on helping entrepreneurial leadership teams simplify, clarify, and achieve their vision. With decades of experience helping hundreds of entrepreneurs get everything they want from their businesses, he is recognized as an expert in the field of leadership team alignment, culture development, and employee engagement.

The product of an entrepreneurial household, Alex has spent much of his business experience focused on his passion for being a Hero to Entrepreneurs. Between selling handmade James Dean t-shirts out of his locker in high school to becoming an Expert EOS Implementer, he ran or helped run four growing businesses. As an Expert EOS Implementer, EOS Community Leader, and co-founder of the EOS Conference®, author, and creator of ProfitWorks, Alex is devoted to helping entrepreneurs both master the Entrepreneurial Operating System (EOS) as well as develop cultures of employees who think and act like owners.

In his free time, Alex enjoys traveling and sharing adventures with his wife, Christine, and three children, Alec, Sophia, and Ethan.

Bonus: Chapter 1 from *Profit Works*

Since 1996, when we first founded ProfitWorks, we have asked employees, "What percent of sales do you think profit is?" Their answers may surprise you; most employees think bottom line profit is 30-50% of sales! While those results would certainly be wonderful, they are not common for most businesses. Upon seeing their employees' answers, one business owner exclaimed, "Are they out of their minds? Do they think I have a money tree in the backyard that I just shake when I want to make more money?"

If your experience is like ours, you know that profit percentages are usually in the single digits, and that profit is incredibly precious. Unfortunately, most employees don't think about this fact as much as you do. They certainly don't see profit numbers as often as you do, if at all. They don't feel connected to profits, and they commonly believe profit is something only the owner or executives need to worry about. Profit is powerful, though, because it funds growth, provides investors and owners with a return, and creates opportunities for employees.

You may have heard profit referred to as the "score at the end of the game." The comparison of business to a game makes it fun and accessible for everyone involved in a company. The game metaphor makes profit that first-place trophy that stretches you and your team. The potential for profit can encourage a competitive spirit and the potential for everyone in a company to win (does anyone like to lose?). The fact that profit is typically small, hard to generate, and easy to lose creates what we call positive tension.

Positive tension is that level of anxiety where people are most productive and motivated. The objectives are not so overwhelmingly difficult or unachievable that no one tries. Conversely, they are not so easy that no one cares or puts in any effort. Think about if you tried out for an NFL team: making the team is probably not going to happen and as a result, you're not going to be motivated. (Well, you might be motivated to avoid getting hurt.)

> Positive tension is that level of anxiety where people are most productive and motivated.

Alternatively, think about your state's DMV: there is no motivation because there is no tension, pressure, or anxiety. Each of you will need to find that optimal level of positive tension in your company. Focusing everyone on profit is a great way to do that.

Profit Works for Everyone

Profit works for owners and investors. The potential for profit creates positive tension to generate a return on investment for investors, relative to the risk they have taken. If there is no profit potential, investors typically won't take the risk to invest in the opportunity.

Profit works for your external relationships. It creates tension for you as it pulls against what it costs you to provide your products and services. It stretches you to make smart decisions related to your sourcing relationships as well as to the investments you make to grow your company through innovation, geographic expansion, and new product and/or service development.

Profit works for your employees. When focused on profit, you have the opportunity to create that right level of tension and to increase opportunities for all of your employees (e.g., advancement, learning new skills, increased compensation). When focused on profit, your entire workforce can benefit by understanding this tension. It can create an incredible culture of winning where everyone is focused on generating more profit.

In addition, we've found that companies win when their employees understand how they benefit from being part of a profitable company; they will see the source of new jobs, the opportunities for reinvestment in the business, and their own potential for growth. We've also found that employees are more motivated when they understand the consequences due to a *lack of* profit, from reductions in force (RIFs) to pay cuts to fewer opportunities for professional growth.

Successful companies understand the benefits of creating positive tension or pressure. Tension isn't a bad thing. According to the Yerkes-Dodson Law, performance increases with tension, but only up to a point. When the level of stress becomes too high, performance decreases. So, a moderate amount of tension creates the most buy-in and effort and, therefore, the most productivity. Like a rubber band, you want to stretch your team to grow and reach for something more than mediocrity. Believe it or not, most people want this.

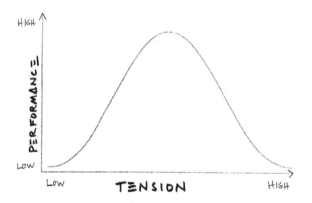

Instilling just enough tension in your culture encourages a higher level of performance. You and your team win when you implement simple and effective tools like weekly meetings full of intense debate and discussion on company issues, and when everyone is accountable. When there's just enough tension in your company, no anchors hold you back from higher performance.

Creating tension in your culture is a blend of art and science. The art is in what tools you decide to teach and how you choose to use those tools. The science comes from using a simple and transparent formula when you design your incentive plan.

Over and over again in client sessions, we hear executives discussing budgeting for bonuses, creating profit-sharing programs, and trying to figure out how to pay employees more so they don't leave for more pay elsewhere. In many cases, though, they're just winging it. There's no clear strategy or methodology for the design. It's often too complicated, not transparent, and has a high degree of subjectivity to it. You may be afraid to draw a line in the sand. You're often shooting from the hip. When incentives aren't truly "earned" and clearly understood, you create an entitlement mentality in your workforce. Entitlement is the death knell for a thriving culture and higher organizational performance.

One of our clients didn't want to follow a formula because she said it might "trap" her. She didn't want to reward under-performing employees. Our question was: "Why are they still with your company?" In the following chapters, we'll give you ideas on how to avoid feeling "trapped."

We encourage you to embrace the intentional philosophies and formulas we share with you in this book. We're capitalists with decades of experience working with hundreds of companies. We've seen what works and what doesn't work. Like you, we want your employees to add more value, to be happy, to be productive, and to earn more, and not to get a bigger paycheck for no real reason.

Before we go further, let's provide an example of a simple incentive plan design that works:

- Imagine an annual profit trigger of $1,000,000. Above this amount, the employees can make more by participating in an incentive pool funded by their efforts. Below this, there's no incentive payout.

- Let's say 30% of every dollar above the $1,000,000 trigger goes into the incentive pool. If the company hits $1,500,000 in profits for the year, the incentive pool is $150,000 (30% x $500,000). It can be as simple as that. We'll talk about some ideas for how that gets distributed later.

COMPANY PROFIT (TRIGGER = $1,000,000)	INCENTIVE POOL (30%)	COMPANY PROFIT (AFTER PAYOUT)
$1,000,000	$0	$1,000,000
$1,500,000	$150,000	$1,350,000

Key Takeaways

- Most employees think bottom line profit is 30-50% of sales.

- Profit is the score at the end of the game and when everyone is focused on profit, you can create positive tension.

- Successful companies create just the right amount of positive tension in their cultures to create higher levels of performance.

- Successful companies commit to a simple formula when designing an incentive plan.

Thinking Questions

These are questions to help you slow down and reflect on what you read as well as to help you think about where your head is on the topics discussed in this chapter.

1. What do you think your employees would guess bottom line profit is as a percentage of sales in your company?

   _____

   _____

   _____

2. What are three examples of positive tension practices you've implemented in your personal life?

   _____

   _____

   _____

3. What changes in your own behavior and thinking have you seen as a result?

   _____

   _____

   _____

ProfitWorks

READY TO CREATE YOUR NO-ENTITLEMENT INCENTIVE PLAN®?

Simple.

Our incentive plans and training programs are designed to be simple to explain, understand, and administer.

Self-Funded.

Employees become active participants in finding incremental profit to fund their incentive plan. With this, the payouts from the incentive plan are earned compensation and not an entitlement.

Supported.

We actively coach Leadership Teams and Program Champions to ensure they are confident to execute the program effectively.

ProfitWorksLLC.com

Want Alex to Keynote your next event?

Let's Connect!

AlexFreytag.com/Speaking

Printed in the USA
CPSIA information can be obtained
at www.ICGtesting.com
LVHW010136080224
771032LV00001B/1/J